Praise for *Dedicant, Devotee, Priest*

"So often we hear of magickal practitioners and pagans yearning for a book that will take them to the next level in their practice. Woodfield has finally answered that call, taking the reader not up some hierarchical ladder, but deep into the heart of creating meaningful relationship with deity. The author distinguishes the difference between devotee and dedicant and explores the question of the daunting and demanding role of what it actually means to call oneself priest/ess. Dedicant, Devotee, Priest is packed not only with useful exercises and ritual, but with sound practical advice from a highly experienced longtime practitioner. Highly recommended for all levels of spiritual practice."

—Danielle Blackwood, Author of *The Twelve Faces of the Goddess* and *A Lantern in the Dark*

DEDICANT
DEVOTEE
PRIEST

© Linda Wilson Photography

about the author

Stephanie Woodfield (Orlando, FL) has been a practicing Pagan for the past twenty years. A devotional polytheist, teacher, and Priestess of the Morrigan, she is one of the founding members of Morrigu's Daughters and is an organizer for several Pagan gatherings. Stephanie teaches classes on devotional work and magical practice in the US and internationally. She resides in the Orlando area with her husband, a very pampered cat, and various reptiles. In her spare time, she enjoys creating art out of skulls and other dead things. She is called to help others forge meaningful experiences with the Morrigan, as well as with the Gods and land of Ireland.

A PAGAN GUIDE TO DIVINE RELATIONSHIPS

DEDICANT
DEVOTEE
PRIEST

STEPHANIE WOODFIELD

Llewellyn Publications • Woodbury, Minnesota

First Edition
First Printing, 2021

Cover design by Shannon McKuhen
Editing by Rosemary Wallner

Llewellyn Publications is a registered trademark of Llewellyn Worldwide Ltd.

Library of Congress Cataloging-in-Publication Data
Names: Woodfield, Stephanie, author.
Title: Dedicant, devotee, priest : a pagan guide to divine relationships /
  Stephanie Woodfield.
Description: First edition. | Woodbury, Minnesota : Llewellyn Worldwide,
  Ltd, 2021. | Includes bibliographical references.
Identifiers: LCCN 2021036810 (print) | LCCN 2021036811 (ebook) | ISBN
  9780738766669 | ISBN 9780738766805 (ebook)
Subjects: LCSH: Paganism. | Spirituality. | Priests.
Classification: LCC BL432 .W66 2021 (print) | LCC BL432 (ebook) | DDC
  299/.94—dc23
LC record available at https://lccn.loc.gov/2021036810
LC ebook record available at https://lccn.loc.gov/2021036811

Llewellyn Worldwide Ltd. does not participate in, endorse, or have any authority or responsibility concerning private business transactions between our authors and the public.

All mail addressed to the author is forwarded but the publisher cannot, unless specifically instructed by the author, give out an address or phone number.

Any internet references contained in this work are current at publication time, but the publisher cannot guarantee that a specific location will continue to be maintained. Please refer to the publisher's website for links to authors' websites and other sources.

Llewellyn Publications
A Division of Llewellyn Worldwide Ltd.
2143 Wooddale Drive
Woodbury, MN 55125-2989
www.llewellyn.com

Printed in the United States of America

Other Books by Stephanie Woodfield

Priestess of the Morrigan

Dark Goddess Craft

Celtic Lore & Spellcraft of the Dark Goddess

Dedication

For Cori. I will always miss your big squishy hugs,
your smile, and your outrageously loud and joyful laughter.
The world is a lesser place without your light in it.

Contents

The Path of Devotion

It is dark in the small building we are using as a temple. There are altars with lit candles and twinkling lights, statues, and bowls full of offerings lining one wall of the room. Chalk symbols are drawn on the floor near the entranceways and on the building itself. Some are small, and you might not even notice what they are if you didn't know what to look for. Our temple is warded, and the presence of the gods has been invited in. There is a comfortable feeling of connectedness that I bask in as I stand here in the dark.

I make my offerings; I say the words I have been using to trigger trance for the last nine months as we have prepared for this work as a group. I pull the veil over my head, and I let the divine fill me. I am still there somewhere, floating as if in a dream. But I don't know what I say to those who enter this space. I am vaguely aware of touching someone's hand, their face. I think a friend of mine has come to speak to the oracle, but I am not sure. What I am the most aware of is the presence of the divine. Holding that vastness within me, blending it with my own energies, yet still keeping a clear and solid sense of self. The me that is me is *consumed completely with holding that presence and doing things like breathing, things gods don't always remember one needs to do. The temple guardian leads people into the space. She checks to make sure that the vessel, the me that is speaking with the voice of the gods, doesn't fall over. That I am safe, that the energy of the temple and its wards remain intact.*

When I come out of trance, I think about how I have felt when I was the one coming to seek answers from the oracle. When I was in the shoes of those who have come seeking, rather than like tonight being the vessel of the gods. Both sides of the experience are profound. I think about how vital it is that we speak to our gods. That we hear their voices. That we learn how to hear them and be heard. So much of our spirituality is about communion with the gods. It is about speaking with the gods to gain connection, wisdom, purpose, and counsel. The last nine months of oracular work for this gathering have been all about just that. The many hours we have taken as a group to create the space of this temple to invite the presence of our gods, and all the protections and steps we have taken to make that process meaningful and smooth. But trance and ritual aren't the only times we commune with the gods, at least they shouldn't be.

Talking to the gods isn't easy. It's something I have been learning to do from my very earliest years in Paganism. The path changed over time. One does not become a priest all at once after all. It began with devotion to the many gods I honor. Then slowly it changed shape into a relationship of deep dedication and service. Even how I served and honored the gods changed over time, just as my understanding of them changed. Walking this path has changed me at the very core. It is not something that happens overnight. It takes a lot of work, but the rewards are invaluable, because I can't imagine being Pagan and not having that connection to the divine. It is, and I'm sure will remain, the most crucial and impactful part of my spiritual journey and work.

From my very first introduction to magic and Paganism, my personal practices have always been very centered on connecting and building deep relationships with the gods and other spirits. Yet while the gods were my focus, admittedly I found it difficult to find the connection I wanted. I found Witchcraft in my early teens. I practiced with various groups, then became solitary for many years to forge my own path with the gods. I had several very profound experiences with deity, but no one could really navigate me through those experiences. Their expertise and practices were focused on magic, rather than deity.

While I have a devotion to many deities, it was the Morrigan who stepped forward as the one that overshadowed the rest, with her guiding my steps for working with the other gods that showed up in my life. I didn't know how to do devotional work. I could cast a circle, I was skilled at magic, but talking to a goddess? Worshiping a deity? I had no clue. It sounds so easy, doesn't it? But there was no manual for how to go about devotional practice, no one to tell me what to avoid or what to try. Now after over twenty years of being a practicing Pagan I find that the majority of what I am asked to teach, or am sought out for, revolves around how to build a connection with the divine. It is one of the things many Pagans feel they were never given the proper toolkit for. I hope to remedy that.

We are told the gods exist, that they can be called on for aid in magic, but that is kind of it. Most Neo-Paganism is based on theurgy, or invoking the divine or other spirits for aid in magic, and at times self-improvement. The problem is theurgy isn't the same as worship. Many times, a deity is only called upon for accomplishing a specific task, offerings are made, gratitude given, and you kind of part ways. I've certainly done the same. It's not that there is anything wrong with theurgy; it just wasn't the fulfilling religious experience I wanted. It felt more like a business transaction than worshiping a god and being in awe of a higher power. Magic was part of my religion, but it was just a tool, not the defining aspect of my spirituality. I needed something more. For a long time, my path felt like stumbling around in the dark trying to find my way and learning how to hear the voices of the gods. So, I listened to the gods for inspiration. I made mistakes, lots of them, and eventually met others who shared my devotion and dedication.

Eventually as my relationship with the Morrigan deepened, I went through several levels of dedications to her. I didn't consider at the time how powerful oaths are. It wasn't that I didn't mean what I vowed to the gods, I very much did, but it changed the relationship. Much like how a relationship might change when you go from casual dating to living with someone. There were different nuances to the relationships, different expectations. Similarly, I found this with the other gods I had a devotional relationship to as well. There are some who will always have honored spaces in my home, and our relationship is simply that of respect, gratitude, and worship. Then there are others that I have specific ties to that bind me to them, specific agreements. They are no less worshiped and honored, but once you have made any kind of agreement or vow to a deity, it becomes a new type of devotion to navigate. There are reasons why heroes and kings in mythology meet untimely ends when they break vows to the gods.

There is a great deal written about magic, how to formulate rituals, but there is very little written about devotional practice, worship, or priesthood. For many the lines between being a ceremonialist and a priest/ess is often blurred and are thought of as the same thing. While a priest may lead a ritual, that is not what defines priesthood. I know many amazing ritualists who do not consider themselves priests. I know many people who are incredibly talented at magic, and yet find it difficult to connect and speak with the gods. Because while they are great ritualists, excellent magicians, they are not priests. Magic is their focus rather than the divine. And that's ok. But we also need to know how to navigate our relationships with the divine.

What is also perhaps a little disturbing is the idea that if you have a strong connection to a deity you are instantly a priest of that deity. Priesthood is complicated and isn't for everyone, nor should it be thrust on someone simply because they have a strong relationship with their gods. There are levels in between that are legitimate kinds of devotion and dedication that are just as meaningful. Furthermore, being a priest/ess is often seen as "leveling up" as a Pagan. That it is the next natural step in one's path. I can tell you it is not. Being a Pagan doesn't mean that you must at some point become a priest/ess. The path of priesthood is just that, a path, one form of devotion, not an end game. If that were true, we would be the first and only religion to consist solely of priests and no laypeople. I don't think priesthood is for everyone, and there is no shame in that. You don't have to be a priest to have a deep and meaningful relationship to the gods. I know many devotees of the Morrigan who consider themselves on a warrior's path or feel called to serve her as a seer. They don't consider themselves priests, but their dedication to her is still both meaningful and full of purpose. Building a devotion isn't always the same as serving as a priest. To some extent in the Pagan community if you have a deep devotion to a deity it is automatically assumed you must be a priest of said deity. Yet those who do find the gods to be central to their worship may not feel called to take on the roles and demands of priesthood. I think we have forgotten that there is a middle ground. That building a devotional practice to the gods is a path and art unto itself.

This is not a book about organizing a coven, group dynamics, or how to host rituals. All the things you have probably been led to believe that are the fundamentals of a being a priest or priestess. Instead this is a book about something that is at the very core of Pagan practice. It is about devotion to the gods, it's about worshiping the gods and yes, priesthood and the paths that lead one there. Devotion and dedication to the gods is a winding path. You don't get there all at once, and you may start out thinking your calling is that of priesthood, only to find along the way that your devotional work takes on a different expression.

Navigating the Branches of Devotion: Or How to Use This Book

I hope this book will be the road map I didn't have when I first started on my path with the gods. Also, I hope for it to serve as a guide for those who wish to build a deeper connection to the divine beings they worship. When I look back at my own journey, I see there were three distinct parts to my path, and so you will find this book divided into three sections: Devotee, Dedicant, and Priest. Each is a different kind of devotion and commitment. Devotee is a foundation in building a devotional practice, which can be useful to anyone wishing to connect with the gods, regardless of being a priest. Dedicant is about how our relationships with the gods change when we make oaths and form alliances with patron deity. Lastly is Priest, where we will look at what being a priest is and isn't, and how to navigate this kind of dedication.

I suggest reading all three sections, but to what degree you take your own personal practices and dedication is entirely up to you. You may find you are only meant to be a dedicant of a deity and not a priest. You may already be a priest and find new dimensions to the work you are already doing. Or you may just wish to learn how to speak with the gods and invite them into your life. No matter what level of devotion you want to explore, there is something here for everyone. It is also important to know where your path might lead. Even if you are not, for example, dedicated to a deity, there is still value in reading that section and understanding the process.

Perhaps you have just started your journey, or you may have been following the winding road a long time. Regardless, devotion is an ever-deepening experience and a path we are never truly done walking. Perhaps the biggest pitfall in any spiritual journey is the illusion that there is always another level to attain. That we are never truly spiritual *enough* until we take that class or attain that certification, attunement or degree, etc. In Western culture especially we are always anticipating the next achievement, the next promotion, the next merit badge or trophy. It's not unlike a video game addict wanting to unlock the next big thing in the game. Upward mobility is something we are taught to seek and see as an accomplishment. Not surprisingly this has translated into Western occultism as well.

We find the same mentality in Wicca and Traditional Witchcraft. Both Gerald Gardner and Aleister Crowley, whose influence on modern Witchcraft as it is practiced today cannot be overstated, drew their practices heavily from the Golden Dawn. Systems like the Golden Dawn, OTO (Ordo Templi Orientis), and anything rooted in ceremonial magic are all based on a degree system. Not surprisingly most traditions of Wicca or Witchcraft also have a three-degree system. For the majority of Pagans, Wicca or Traditional Witchcraft is the only Pagan system they are familiar with, and we tend to fall into the mindset that as we grow spiritually and progress in our spirituality, we will climb up the degree system. This is a mindset that we must break. Deeper understanding of something, spiritual or otherwise, is not directly proportional to how many titles or degrees as an occultist or Pagan you have.

It's very important to not see this journey into the heart of devotion as an upward climb. We are not climbing a mountain to its summit. That sort of journey has an end goal, planting the flag at the top and then the journey is over. Instead think of this as the branches on a tree. You need all the branches for the tree to be healthy and stable, and you may roost on one branch for a while, then climb to another. Some branches are parallel, others bring you in different directions. You may find you climb between branches or find one that supports your spiritual needs and callings the most. You may find only one path appealing, or you may find all three paths outlined in this book familiar places within your journey.

I encourage you to read each section so you have a foundation in each aspect of devotional practice, but do so with the understanding that you are only obligated to find what fits you and your needs the most. Not every devotee will be a priest, yet every priest is a devotee. Or you may find yourself navigating the rewards and pitfalls of a dedication to a deity for several years before you take on the mantel of priesthood. Don't rush, take your time. You may climb up and down the tree a while before finding your place on it. We are not climbing a mountain, but instead putting down strong roots and reaching up towards the gods.

Terminology

Most of the terms I use in this book for divine or semi-divine beings are "god/s," "goddess," and "deity." But the beings we traditionally think of as gods aren't the only beings one might worship or seek building a connection with. While I use these terms in a broad sense, they in no way exclude the ancestors, the fair folk, demigods, angelic or celestial beings, land spirits, spirits of place, or anything else you can think of. It is simply unproductive to name out every kind of being you can connect with in any situation. So, while I might use the term "deity," feel free to insert in its place whatever beings or spirits you have a connection to.

Journaling

Journaling can be a valuable tool when we start the practice of communing and speaking with the gods. How you do it doesn't really matter, just that you do it consistently. I personally hate traditional journaling. I'm more of a note taker. If writing out long paragraphs explaining your thoughts and feelings works best for you, that is great. It's only one way to journal. Bullet points with short descriptions and thoughts are perfectly valid as well. If you have ever done a science experiment or brewed mead you know how important note taking is. This is sort of like that. Just the mead you are brewing is your connection to deity. Having a notebook to look back on your steps will help you in the long run. You can see where you made mistakes, what worked and what didn't. If you took good notes, you might be able to isolate the reasons why something worked better or worse for you.

Many of the techniques in this book require that you build a long-term practice. Whether it is prayer, oracular work, or daily devotions, they will not be something you do just once. They won't be things that are perfect the first time or even the twentieth time you do them. It's an evolving practice and it's important to document it and build a resource for you to use. Many of the things in this book will also challenge you to think about what the gods are or how you feel about different ideas and practices. Your ideas about these things will more than likely grow the longer you are doing this work. And that's perfectly ok. If some of your ideas didn't change you wouldn't be evolving. Journaling helps us organize those ideas and work through them.

Traditions & Paths

I try to cover the perspectives of as many paths and points of view as possible throughout. The deities I mention are ones I have a personal relationship with, and in no way limit the scope of the pantheons or beings one can use these practices with. These techniques can be used effectively regardless of the tradition or path you are a part of. Whether you are part of an initiatory tradition or lean towards a more eclectic spirituality should also have no bearing on using any of the information in this book. I try to use examples from the traditions I have the most experience and background in. Examples of many of the things discussed exist in other traditions, but out of respect, I do not wish to speak for traditions I am not a part of.

Suggested Exercises

At the end of each chapter there is a list of suggested exercises. In part one they are more hands on, while in parts two and three they are more introspective to help you refine your own devotional work. I suggest you work through the exercises at your own pace; don't rush through them. These are all excellent topics to journal about, or keep some kind of record, so you can look back on your progress and what has worked for you and what hasn't.

Devotee

A devotee is someone who has a strongly held belief in a god, religion, or faith. We find followers of this kind of spiritual devotion in all religions. Whether you are a Christian, Hindu, or Neo-Pagan, if you seek to draw a deity's presence into your life, engage in prayer, or have an altar, you are a devotee of whatever god or spirit you honor or seek a connection with. The defining aspects of the path of a devotee is *devotion* and building a relationship with the gods. How you build that connection can happen in many ways, which we will explore in depth in this section. No matter how you get there, the end result is the same. When you have built a devotional relationship with a deity, they become a part of your life. Not just your magical and ritual life, but a presence you can call on in your darkest moments, at work, or in the car when you are just having a bad day. Once that bridge has been built between devotee and deity, they will speak to you and come into your life at times you may least expect but need it the most. It is not a one-way line of communication.

Being a devotee differs from the path of a dedicant or priest in that there are no strings attached, so to speak. You can be a devotee of a god or goddess but not have any formalized oaths or agreements to that deity. This isn't to say you can't have a deep relationship with that being; it's just one level of connection. While all priests are devotees of a deity or spirit of some kind, priesthood's primary function does not revolve around you. In short it is not about you, it's about service. Devotion, on the other hand, revolves primarily around you and your own personal work with the divine. Another way to approach it is to think of it in terms of the relationship you have with your friends, versus something more intimate like a marriage. Both are relationships, with different levels of responsibility, connection, and intimacy. Friendship can come and go and have fewer formal agreements attached to the ways you interact or how long the relationship lasts.

CHAPTER ONE

What Is a Deity?

The lake we are visiting is quite beautiful. Lough Gur is roughly horseshoe-shaped, and today it reflects the sunlight like a mirror. A tall green hill rises up behind it, and I immediately feel the urge to climb up it. It all looks like something out of a fairy tale, and I am reminded that in a way it is. In folklore a local Earl was said either to have been the lover of Áine, the goddess and sometimes faery queen, or to have forced himself upon her. He is either sleeping or imprisoned below the lake, coming to the surface every seven years to try to return to this world. Of course, he can't, not until the silver on his shoes wears thin enough to break the spell. One of our group does indeed stand too close to the edge of the lake and somehow the ground beneath her gives way and she falls in. I am reminded that once lost in faery it is hard to get out again, and that both faery queens and goddesses can be equally dangerous when angered.

We continue on the path, but it starts to veer away from the green hill of Knockadoon. There is no clear path towards the hill that we can see, so while some of our group continues on the path

a few of us hop over a wooden fence and attempt to climb the hill.
I get about halfway up before I stop, out of breath. I am also con-
sidering how long it will take to get back down and to our tour
bus in time for our departure. But the view is still as spectacular
as I could have hoped, and I take some time to reach out and con-
nect with the energy of the land. It's all too beautiful to close my
eyes, so I let my sight wander and meditate while I gaze at the
land around me. I can feel Áine here. Her presence is very palpa-
ble, more so than I thought it would be. There is something else
too. The fairy folk feel highly active here. I have always thought of
Áine more as a goddess than a faery queen. I had always assumed
faery queen was a role she was assigned later on, as a way to
diminish her power as a goddess. I wonder if being a faery queen
is any less powerful than being a goddess? Are they the same? Dif-
ferent? Does it matter? What is a god anyway? Other than just
a word we use to try to encompass the vast powers of greater
beings? I am wondering if there really is a hard line where one
can be distinguished from the other. Because here in this place the
energy of Áine and the sidhe, the fair folk, are so intermingled I
cannot help but think of her as a faery queen now. After coming
to this place, now Áine without the sidhe is not Áine in my mind
anymore. Yet she is no less powerful. As the thought goes through
my mind, something small and brown dashes through the long
grass in front of me. It looks back when I do not move, and I see
it's a large hare. It stands up on its hind legs and considers me for
a moment then dashes off again. I take it as a good sign. Maybe
there is no difference at all: Áine is just Áine, no matter what I call
her or think she is.

What is a deity? At first glance this may seem obvious, but depending on what pantheon, spiritual path, or tradition you are a part of, the answer can be vastly different. So, before we look at how we can build a devotional practice with a deity, it's important to understand what exactly we are worshiping, honoring, or connecting with in the first place.

When we come from monotheistic religions into Paganism, we often bring with us certain ideas about divinity. We may change the name of the deity we are worshiping, or perhaps the gender, but often we retain the basic concepts we have been taught about what a god, no matter the name, actually is. One such automatic assumption is that the definition of a god is an all-powerful spirit who created humanity, the earth, the universe and everything in it. Perhaps not surprisingly that is not the definitive definition of a god in all religions. While in some pantheons a grouping of gods, or usually a specific god creates the world and/or humankind, not all deities are considered all-powerful. Specialized power is most commonplace. A deity will have a powerful influence over a specialized skill set or aspect of existence. They are certainly enormously powerful beings, but many times have limits. So, one would pray to a god of healing or medicine for healing sickness, and god of war for overcoming obstacles, etc. One wouldn't pray to a god of chaos or a trickster deity, for example, for a good harvest, any more than you would go to a carpenter when you need surgery. In some cases, the gods even share mortal qualities, such as the gods of the Irish pantheon who have a habit of dying in one story only to appear whole and reformed in the next story. They die, a very mortal trait, yet they are so powerful they transcend it easily. Similarly, in Greek mythology the gods have similar issues as their mortal counterparts and have very human emotions that drive them. They experience jealousy, love, anger. They have affairs, fall in love, make mistakes, and have grudges with one another.

In the Shinto religion there are various levels of beings, all of which are called Kami. Yet the Kami range from anything from a minor spirit or faery to what we would consider in the Western world to be a full-fledged god. Amaterasu, the well-known Japanese sun goddess, is one such Kami. We in the West call her a goddess because that is where she falls in the Western concept of divinity, but in the context of the culture she comes from she is one of the Kami. The understanding is that there is a hierarchy among these beings. Amaterasu is simply a being on the top tier of the hierarchical system.

Another example to consider are the Irish sidhe, or faeries. In the *Lebor Gabála Érenn* or *The Book of Invasions* which chronicles the many different races of divine beings who invaded Ireland, we are told the Tuatha De Danann (the Irish pantheon of gods) eventually retreat into the faery mounds when the ancestors of mortal men arrive on the island. Many sacred places in Ireland are held to be sacred to particular Irish deities, as well as being a place inhabited and connected to the sidhe. Some Irish gods were later reduced to faery kings and queens in folklore. The goddess Áine retains her status as a goddess but is also considered a faery queen as well, blurring the lines further. So, are the Irish gods actually "gods"? Or are they the fair folk? This is a question often debated amongst those who practice Irish spirituality.

I think perhaps we are looking at the question backwards. The places held sacred to the Irish gods and the sidhe are often the same. They both are thought to inhabit the realms of the Other-

worlds. The lines blur perhaps because what I suspect we are looking at is a hierarchy of beings, not unlike the Kami, with what we
consider faeries on the lower level of the spectrum and the Tuatha
De Danann on the topmost tier, making them gods in our eyes.
Both have been worshiped and both have power, just varying levels
of power and abilities. I don't think this makes the Irish gods any
less gods, but when we consider what is and isn't a deity it is perhaps better to not draw hard lines and take a more fluid approach.

To make it ever more complicated, there are many people who
have a devotional relationship with the sidhe, animal spirits, the
ancestors, angelic beings, spirit guides, and all sorts of beings we
may not consider to be gods. They are no less devotees of these
beings and powers, but it does require that we take time to consider what we define a god to be. Not everyone's definition will be
the same, nor does it need to be. Furthermore, many people may
enter into a devotional relationship with spirits and beings that
they do not consider gods, and that is perfectly valid as well. There
are a variety of beings we can enter into devotional relationships
with that are mutually beneficial.

For the purposes of this book while I use the words "god/dess"
and "deity," I am making no hard or fast assumptions about what
those terms mean to you the reader. If you are seeking a devotional relationship with the sidhe, archangel Michael, Coyote, your
ancestors, the Jötunn, or Kali, the process is the same.

I do suggest you take some time and consider your own criteria
and viewpoint on what is and isn't a deity. How have your views
evolved and changed? What changed them? Very often people fall
into the trap of needing to be "right." I can say from experience
that your views on the gods will evolve and change the longer

you have a devotional relationship with them. That is ok, let your beliefs evolve and change. You are allowed to say: "I once thought this, and now I think differently." That is actually a good thing, because it means you are growing, and so is your understanding of the divine. Perhaps when you started your path or were at a certain stage in your journey you weren't ready to understand something about the gods you honor for whatever reason. In the Morrigan community, you will find a lot of quibbles fought over whether or not the Morrigan is one goddess, three individual sisters with one shared title, and so on. I could tell you what the stories and lore say about that. I could tell you what I thought when I first started working with her, and the completely different ideas I have now after almost twenty years in her service. I can also tell you that all of those points of view are correct at the same time. There is no black and white, yes or no, answer. We aren't meant to have all the answers when we first start out. And honestly, I don't think we in our mortal incarnated forms can handle true understanding of a deity's nature any more than an ant can conceptualize what my day is like. In many cultures and religions, it is thought that seeing the true form and splendor of a deity would incinerate a mortal. So, think of it as if we are seeing just the edge of that brilliance, muted and shadowed so that we can make sense of it in this incarnation. I don't think any of us can understand the full scope of deity while in our current form.

Attributes of Deity

As we can see not everyone attributes the same powers or qualities to every kind of deity. Even within a given pantheon, the abilities and powers of a deities can vary. When looking across religions we have everything ranging from beings with specific niche powers, to all-powerful and all-knowing deities, to incarnated human beings who have been deified. Add to that the fact that even those who worship the same deity can have vastly different views on what exactly that deity is within the grander scheme of things. One person who worships Thor may simply view him as an ancestral spirit, another might view Thor as an omnipotent being, and yet another may feel he is omnipresent but not omnipotent. In order to delve more deeply into what a deity is, we then must look at some of the characteristics and concepts surrounding godhood. Hopefully looking at each of these attributes will help you think about your own viewpoints on deity. Many of these attributes are extremes and you might find yourself viewing the gods in a grey area or middle area on many of these topics. The point is to really look at what you believe and why you believe it. What do these beliefs mean to you as a worshiper of a particular deity? How do they shape your practices and your approach? How do they shape your perception of the world?

Omnipotent

Omnipotence refers to a deity that is all-powerful. They can literally create or do anything and have no limitations whatsoever. This usually refers to a singular being. Although at times there may be a singular omnipotent deity within a pantheon, that is the creator of other gods who are less powerful than itself. We are perhaps the most familiar with this concept from Christianity, where there is a singular all-powerful deity. But this isn't actually a purely Judeo-Christian idea. In Egypt, the pharaoh Akhenaton transformed the religious landscape of his empire by promoting the worship of Aton (sometimes spelled Aten) as a singular and all-powerful solar deity, opposing the longstanding worship of a hierarchy of gods who ruled over distinct areas of expertise. It was a movement that didn't last very long in Egyptian history, but it does clearly show that the concept is not unique to Christianity. Aristotle talks about a similar concept which he calls the Unmoved Mover. Aristotle's Unmoved Mover is an eternal being without form that is responsible for all the change and motion in the universe yet is unmoving itself. Think about a moth that is attracted to a lightbulb. The lightbulb is attracting the moth and is the cause for its motion and actions; the lightbulb is itself not moving, but it is the reason for all the movements of the moth around it.

Distinct Dominion

This is the opposite of omnipotent. A deity may have vast power, but it is specialized. We see this in many of the pantheons around the world where deities are categorized based on what segment of reality they have sway over. There are deities of agriculture, love, wealth, war, and so on. Each has a great deal of power compared to us, but it is a specific area of expertise instead of supreme power over all things.

Immutable

An immutable deity is one that does not change. Within Christianity this is usually understood to go hand in hand with the idea of the perfection of god. Deity does not change simply because it is already perfect, and possesses perfect wisdom, knowledge, and grace. It also insinuates that the deity likewise cannot be changed by its own creations or affected by them in any way. Within Paganism you may often see the debate about whether or not a deity can appear to a worshiper in modern-day clothing. What is being argued here really is whether a deity can change. Are they stuck in time, or have they existed in distilled perfection from the beginning of time and remain in that frozen state? If a deity is not immutable it can also insinuate that their area of expertise can change and evolve. For example, many modern worshipers of the Morrigan see her ruling over self-sovereignty, a concept that really did not exist in Ireland during her worship. This would mean that she is not immutable, because she has evolved to suit the needs of the worlds around her and her worshipers. On the flip side you can argue that she embodied all possible forms of sovereignty from the beginning, and that we are only now seeing a side of her that was already there. You can really run in circles with many of these ideas, and again it is up to you to decide for yourself where the gods you honor fall in these categories.

Omnipresent

This is the idea that a deity is present both anywhere and everywhere. You can see this as deity existing within all things. It is also the concept that two people on opposite ends of the world can be talking to the same deity and be given equal attention at the same time. It's the ultimate kind of multitasking. It also reflects the power of a being to be present and interacting everywhere at once without limitation.

Omniscience

This is the idea that a god is all-knowing. It isn't necessarily wisdom although it can be depending on one's view of deity. In Frank

Herbert's *God Emperor of Dune*, his character Leto gains the ability to access all the memories of every human who has every lived, thus gaining a kind of omniscience. But knowing everything doesn't always make one wise; it simply makes them more perceptive. Many times, omniscience is attributed to a particular deity within a pantheon. Primordial gods, gods of wisdom or prophecy, fulfill this function at times.

Benevolent

In general, most religions view their deities as benevolent in some way. In some cases, they may be omnibenevolent, representing limitless and prefect goodness. Usually if a deity is omnibenevolent, they have an opposing deity that is either an antagonist or a balancing force that represents complete evil. We can also see benevolence in stories of gods who create things to help humankind or take an interest in our wellbeing. Prometheus gives humankind the gift of fire, deities of agriculture giving humankind tools and knowledge to cultivate food so there is no starvation, etc. In many cases this benevolence is attributed to deity because we are viewed as their creation, thus attributing their benevolence to a kind of parent-child relationship. This isn't always the case though. Many modern Heathens tend to take the viewpoint that while the gods created humankind, they aren't generally concerned much with us. Instead honoring them and making offerings to the gods brings about their benevolence, rather than a familial obligation just for existing.

The Three Primary Qualities of Deity

As we can see the characteristics of a deity vary quite a bit. When we take into consideration all these often vastly different viewpoints it's hard to find commonalities. Yet there is some common ground. There are three primary qualities to any deity. No matter what deity you are looking at, they will have all three of these qualities in various degrees. Depending on your personal viewpoints and the pantheon/religion in question, your mileage will vary.

Power

This is perhaps the most defining aspect of deity. Gods have power. Power to shape events, to shape reality, to create, etc. How much power a deity has is usually what is debated. Whether a deity is all-powerful with no other force or power being above it, or is just simply more powerful than we are, varies. In general spirits considered gods will have more power that the other beings and spirits found within that cultural context or pantheon. Such as the Aesir (Norse gods) verses dwarfs or elves. All three are spirits within the realm of Heathen belief, yet the Aesir are the most powerful, and this in part is why we call them gods.

Perspective

Perspective can come in many forms. Many cultures place the home of their gods in the sky, on mountains, or in high places. In part this may be because we view gods as having greater perspective than ourselves. From where they dwell, they can see the patterns of reality, cause and effect, the threads of the future in greater detail. It is like the view of someone looking down at a chessboard versus the viewpoint of someone who is on the chessboard itself. If you are looking down at the chessboard you can see the whole playing field, you can see how different pieces can be moved to win the game, and you can see the patterns of game play. If you are a chess piece you can't see the bigger picture; you probably can only see the players directly beside you. Perspective matters. It is in part why we seek the wisdom of the gods because they can see the vastness of the universe in a way we cannot. They see the bigger picture. This perspective can be specialized such as gods of prophecy whose specific purview is viewing the future. Gods of communication, such as Mercury, you could argue specialize in having greater perspective of the present as well.

Timelessness

I do not use the term immortal simply because many divine beings go through a cycle of dying and being reborn in their mythology. Timelessness is instead the idea that time does not touch them. They can die and be reborn and still be untouched by time. In one form or another they are eternal. They continue to exist because they are not constrained by time as we are. It is also the idea that they have always and will always exist, at least from our own perspective. Newgrange and the pyramids are timeless from our own perspective after all. They existed before we were born and will exist after we are gone. They are not immortal in the truest sense but might as well be from our point of view. Whether a god is immortal in the truest sense really does not matter, since as far as we can currently perceive they are.

This can also be said of deities that start off as mortal beings. Jesus, Buddha, even Roman emperors who were deified by the state all began as mortals who became deified. This process of apotheosis can be found in several cultures. The emperor Hadrian deified his lover Antinous after he drowned, and even erected a city named after him on the shores of the river. Despite starting out mortal these figures can attain a kind of timeless immortality.

Suggested Exercises

1. Take some time to journal about your views on deity. How have they changed? Why have they changed?

2. What attributes do you assign to deity? Are they universal to all pantheons, or do they vary from deity to deity?

3. What influences your beliefs? Personal experiences, religious theologies? Journal your thoughts.

CHAPTER TWO

Building a Connection to Deity

I am sitting on my patio watching a falcon that has taken up residence in the wooded area behind my house. I have been seeing it more frequently this last month hunting in our yard. I wish it luck in catching the mice I've seen in our storage shed near the far end of the yard. One day while I am gardening it swoops down not far away and catches a lizard. It perches on a thick low hanging branch picking apart its prize and every so often tilting its head to look at me, as I also watch it.

On the patio my friend and I talk about the event we are going to at a friend's New Age shop. The owner often hosts rituals in the little area behind the store. Usually we are the ones running the rituals but tonight is a treat: someone else is facilitating the ritual and we can simply enjoy the ritual and have less on our shoulders. I check my phone before we get in the car and head to our friend's shop. I notice I'm tagged in a photo. It's a picture of one of my books next to a book written by a friend about Freya. That's the second time I've been tagged in something that had something of my own and something pertaining to Freya this month. I think of the falcon, and the pieces are starting to come together.

We arrive at the shop and find out that the person who was supposed to host the ritual can't make it and the store owner isn't sure what to do as more people arrive. I know of course we are about to be recruited. I silently tell myself I shouldn't have tempted the gods by saying how nice it was to have a night off as priestess. I should know better.

A plan is formed. Which is mostly me suggesting to my fellow priestess that she host a sumbel and I'll play the role of support priestess. I could do something for the Irish gods with little notice. But it doesn't feel right. Often when set plans go awry the gods want us to go in a different direction. I think of the falcon and of Freya. She is trying to talk to me. I could ignore the signs, or I could open a path of communication between us.

The sumbel, which consists of ritualized toasting and hails to ancestors and the gods as well as boasts, goes well. A good number of people are there so we limit it to one round to the ancestors or beloved dead and one to the gods. We have folks who practice various versions of Paganism there as well as other assorted paths. My friend tells them they do not have to limit the gods they hail to the Norse pantheon; we all bring our gods with us wherever we go. It is interesting to see the variety. Norse and Irish, Hindu gods, a faery queen, the Christian god by a woman attending in support of her Pagan husband are all hailed. My husband who is also dedicated to the Morrigan hails the Great Queen, to no one's surprise. He hands the horn to me, and I pause. The Morrigan can be very all-consuming in my life. It's something I'm perfectly *fine with. Yet it does not mean that I don't worship or have devotions to other gods. But it can be daunting opening myself up to and exploring a new connection, when the one to her is so intricate and well worn. It is easy for me to connect to the Morrigan. I forget that in a new relationship I need to feel out my footing along unfamiliar terrain.*

I am only supposed to hail one deity. But I feel Freya there with us, and I feel if I do not recognize her then I will be turning my back on what she is offering me. She has been hailed by others in the circle, but I think she is waiting for me to call to her. For me to welcome her. So, I say there are two gods I must acknowledge. I hail both the Morrigan and Freya together. The Morrigan first to acknowledge agreements already in place, and then Freya whose presence I mention I feel quite strongly among us. I send out my own energetic invitation as well with the words. I see you. I am listening. I welcome you. I feel an acknowledgement of this from Freya as well.

It became easier to connect with her after that. There was more to do certainly, but sometimes we need to welcome the gods in our lives. When they show up, we don't always have to listen. We can choose to turn a blind eye, and many do, not recognizing the gods are calling to them. But the gods showing up in our lives isn't enough to forge a connection to them. We have to reach out to them in welcome too.

How do we learn to hear the voices of the gods? How can we seek to build a devotional relationship with them? Where do we begin? These are the questions most people have when they feel called to honor a deity.

Sometimes we court the gods, and sometimes they court us. Most of us are probably familiar with the idea that a deity might just show up in one's life and turn things upside down to get our attention. But this is not connection. This is a deity trying to make you realize they are there, and they probably have been a presence in your life for some time. Many people find these experiences to be confirmation of a god's existence. On some level it certainly is confirmation, but it is also the godly equivalent of shouting at you. You want to be able to hear their voices and feel their presence in a less disruptive way. On the flip side, you might want to connect with a deity or being and are not getting any noticeable response. Building a connection and relationship to deity is not about big grand gestures, it's about the everyday. It's about how you weave that connection to divinity within your life in a way that nourishes you. That can be something quite difficult.

For a long time, ritual was my only source of connection to the gods. It wasn't because they weren't present or trying to talk to me at other times. I just wasn't listening. I thought the only place I could make that connection was in sacred space. Eventually I realized this was only true because when I did ritual I was concentrating on that connection. Sacred space was all around me if I acknowledged it, and my link to the divine could be too. The gods weren't just around when I did ritual; they were always there.

We learn the mechanics of ritual and magic, but the process of connecting to our gods can seem daunting. Part of the problem is the techniques of magic are easy to replicate. I can tell you to say these words and tie a knot in red string and given enough force of willpower the spell can be replicated fairly regularly and quite successfully. I can also tell you what offerings the Cailleach prefers, but that doesn't mean that if you give her said offering that she will show up when you call. The gods don't work that way. Maybe she doesn't have something to say to you, maybe there are other gods that are calling to you. I can only tell you what has worked for myself and others, but I can't guarantee an experience. That's a bridge you will have to build, between yourself and the divine on your own. So much of devotional work is about your own personal journey. I can give you the guide map, but ultimately what works best for you will depend on you. It will also depend on the gods you build this connection with. Every god or spirit has their own personalities and preferences. Keep in mind what works for one might not be what works for another.

Veneration vs. Working With

The reasons behind any interaction with a power or deity is important to consider. Why are we embarking on creating this relationship? Why do we seek to speak with the divine? An important aspect of this is considering the language we use.

More often than not in Paganism we call any kind of interaction with deity, magical or otherwise, "working with" said deity. Words have power, they set expectations and mindsets even when we don't realize it, and I think using this verbiage to describe our relationships with the gods can be problematic.

We will all have different kinds of relationships with the divine. There may be deities you only call upon for seasonal rituals, or for a magical purpose, for personal development, and others that you have a deep daily connection to. Regardless of the purpose these beings are still greater than ourselves and deserving of respect. You might not have a deep private relationship, like you may have with other deities, but the respect we approach them with should be the same regardless.

The issue I tend to see with using "working with" is that people start relating to the gods as equals. You aren't working with Hekate the same way you work with Sally your co-worker at the office. Hekate is a goddess that helped the world spin into motion, and asking for her aid demands a little more reverence than this term implies. It also insinuates that the gods are only here to be "worked with" to get things. There will be times you ask for aid or guidance, but how you go about asking for aid from an equal is different from the awe and respect owed to greater powers. That may be making offerings, praying or honoring deity in some other way. But not every interaction with deity should be because you want something. You should engage in meditation and prayer, and connect with them simply to build a relationship to them. To praise and yes, worship them.

That being said, I'm totally guilty of using this term and still have to catch myself when using this terminology. Within Paganism we have our own vocabulary and lingo for our practices, and this particular one I think undermines our work with the gods more than anything. When we say "working with" what we usually mean is worship or veneration. If you are only calling on Aphrodite just that one time to give that love spell some extra zing, if you spoke a god's name and asked for their help, praised them in any way and left offerings in thanks, then you are engaging in a form of worship. Even if you don't have a continued relationship with that deity, it is still important to show that respect. Worship when mixed with magic is often referred to as theurgy, but the elements of worship remain the same, regardless of magic being thrown into the mix.

The problem is words like "worship" evoke images of steepled churches and remind people of the bad taste the religions of their childhoods left in their mouths. So, we use new terms, ones we didn't hear growing up. I think there is something to be said about taking back these words, because the Abrahamic religions don't own the copyright on them. Humans have been worshiping everything from trees, rocks, the spirits of the dead, to the fair folk, and a multitude of gods from the very beginning. The concept of worship is a human function. It is how we honor and relate to the spirit world. It applies to Pagans as much as it applies to Christians or Buddhists. If the word worship does leave a sour taste in your mouth, you could always replace it with "devotion" or "veneration" instead.

Learn the Myths and Culture of Who You are Talking To

Yes, I know this is the boring bit. But trust me it will pay off. You cannot worship or understand a deity if you know nothing about them. The more familiar you are with the myths, lore, and culture a deity comes from, the more you will understand their nature. I believe gods evolve and how they may present themselves in the modern world may differ a bit from how they might have in ancient times. Yet if you don't know the things they are associated with, or the things that might insult them based on their worship in the past, you could put your spiritual foot in your mouth very easily. You may also miss omens and messages deity is trying to convey to you if you don't know a particular thing is significant in their stories. The mythology of the gods, their stories and deeds, form a kind of sacred text for those who worship them. Just like a Christian might find meaning and comfort in reading the Bible, or a Muslim the Koran, so too can we find meaning in reading and understanding the stories of our gods.

Spending time learning and reading about deity and keeping them in your thoughts is also a mental way of welcoming them into your life. Like calls to like, and if you keep sending the message into the universe that you want to connect and know about XYZ deity, the more likely you are to have a response. On the flip side, if a deity shows up in your life out of the blue, learning more about them will help you understand why they might have chosen this time to appear in your life.

Once you have read some of the myths and stories connected to the deity in question, you can start using them as a tool for active connection to the divine. I started this practice after attending a talk hosted by a Pagan artist discussing his methodology for creating his pieces. What I found interesting about his work was that even though the figures were recognizable as gods from the Norse pantheon, they very much had his own unique spin on them. They did not depict familiar stories yet conveyed something vital about the deity in other ways. He started off by meditating on a passage from the Hávamál, and afterwards he would start sketching based on the impressions and feelings he got from the meditation. Afterwards I started doing something similar. I would take a short passage from a myth or in some cases one of The Triads of Ireland, which are short sayings on various topics, many of which mention the Irish gods, and used those as my focus for meditation. After the meditation I might journal or write a prayer for the deity I was trying to connect with through the focused meditation. Other times I would try to create something artistic based on what revealed itself in the meditation. What I found was it helped me hone in on the energy of the deity more easily. This was especially helpful for gods I wanted to build a connection to, but I was mostly unfamiliar with. For gods I was already close with, it helped me connect to different aspects of them more deeply and explore different layers to their mythology.

Altars & Places of Worship

Altars are a good way to welcome gods and spirits into your life. They also serve as a place for you to focus your everyday spiritual activities such as making offerings and daily devotions. An altar can be as simple or complex as you want. For those who do not have much space or the funds to buy statues and other decorative items we usually associate with altars, the space you set aside to honor the gods can be as simple as a candle on the kitchen table or an art print on the wall that others might not recognize as anything other than home decor. Whatever way you set up your altar, the important part is to use it. It shouldn't be sitting there collecting dust and only used once or twice a year. Clean and dust it regularly—in short, treat it as a sacred place. To build a connection to deity this should be a place you regularly visit to connect with the divine; make it a place that you regularly make offerings and tend to.

I have often joked that my house is a giant shrine to various gods that I just happen to live in. There are many altars to many different gods. While the Morrigan's altar is the one that most of my practices are focused on, the rest are not ignored. There are certain days of the week, moon cycle, etc. when these altars are tended. For example: Fridays are when I tend Brigid's flame and do devotions on her altar. During storm season in Florida, the Cailleach is given special attention. While during the New Moon, a time when offerings were traditionally given to Hekate, her altar is cleaned and given special attention. Eventually this begins to become a familiar cycle, one you can look forward to, and can tweak to fit your schedule.

Pilgrimages

There is something powerful about visiting a place that has been connected to a deity for hundreds of years. To touch a stone spoken about in a myth that has held meaning to you in your spiritual practices. To be able to connect and stand upon the land named after a deity you honor. Humans have been going on pilgrimages to sacred sites since the very beginning and continue to do so across all religions today.

My understand of the Irish gods deepened significantly after going on pilgrimage to Ireland. Pilgrimages offer a time for you to step away from the everyday and spend time almost exclusively focusing on your spiritual path. The entire trip can be a ritual in itself. Of course, not everyone is going to have the time or money available to travel. But if you cannot go on a literal pilgrimage you can still connect to sacred sites in other ways. Pictures of sacred sites and even videos tours from those who have visited these sites can be found online. Pictures of a sacred site connected to a deity you honor can be printed out and placed on their altar. Or you can use them as a focal point for astral work. Visiting a sacred site through journey work and astral travel is still a legitimate way to connect to the power of these places and the gods associates with them.

Daily Devotions

Daily devotions are specific actions or times in a day specifically set aside to connect with or honor deity. Daily devotions take many forms and can be as simple or elaborate as you like. For some this might be spending a few minutes meditating by an altar and saying a set mantra or prayer. It might be taking a yoga stance while centering one's thoughts on connecting to deity. Whatever form your daily devotions take, the point is that you are taking a few minutes of the day to open yourself to connecting with and honoring the divine. For some this is combined with altar tending, but it doesn't have to be. You can do a devotional anywhere. In front of your altar, in your car, silently at work, etc.

Daily devotions aren't a requirement of worshiping a deity, but it's a good practice to get into. It doesn't make you a bad Pagan if you don't pick up this practice. Everyone has to find what practices are the most meaningful to them. It's just another tool in your toolbox when it comes to connecting to the divine, but also not something you are going to be perfect at. There will inevitably be a day where you are running late, or something interrupts you from being able to do your devotional activity. That's ok. For myself it began as a practice to help me slow down, to make time for deity among the busyness of the day. Eventually it became the part of the day I looked forward to the most, because of the connection with deity that I was fostering.

While other devotional practices might focus on speaking with and receiving information from a deity, daily devotionals aren't done with the intention of receiving anything. This isn't to say that the gods might not use the opportunity to impart something to you; they certainly can. But the intentions you go into your daily devotions with should not start with the thought that you "need" something, whether that be advice or aid, etc. The point is to take time to be present and aware of your relationship and connection with the gods, and to honor their presence in your life.

The easiest way to start out is to pick a prayer you like (or write one) and a time of day to do your devotions. Making it a set routine helps to make it a part of your day that you will look forward to and stick with. Saying, "Well, I'll do it whenever I have time in the day" usually leads to you doing the exercise once or twice then not returning to it. Whatever time you decide, try to stick with it for at least a month. If it's not working, pick a different time and try to stick with that until you find what works best.

If you are incorporating a prayer or mantra into your devotional, you should also take the time to memorize the words. Reading and concentrating on what the next line is takes us out of the headspace we need to be in. The more automatic the words are, the easier it will be for you to be present and feel the presence of deity.

You might also want to incorporate a trigger into your devotions. A trigger is a thing you do, say, or touch that signals your brain that you are going into an altered state. For example, if you hold a particular stone each time you begin your devotionals, eventually simply the act of holding the stone in your hand will trigger you to go into that headspace. Your trigger could be anything you wish. It might be hearing a song. Tracing a symbol on your palm, lighting a certain incense or candle. Eventually the whole ritual of doing your daily devotional can become a trigger itself to enter into a head space to connect to the divine. My own daily devotion consists of saying a prayer and making certain hand gestures during certain lines of that prayer. As soon as I put my hands in that first position, my mind instantly goes into that headspace.

Prayer

Although we will look at this practice in depth in the next chapter, it is worth mentioning that prayer is a powerful tool to connect to the gods. Prayer can also be a part of daily devotionals or as a practice all unto itself. It helps focus our thoughts towards the divine and can be useful to those who need something more concrete to do to connect to the gods, rather than doing energy or meditative work.

Dreams

Everyone connects to the gods differently. Maybe meditation isn't doing it for you, or you aren't getting anywhere with your daily devotions. If that is the case, you can also ask the gods to come to you in your dreams. Learning some lucid dreaming techniques, creating a dream pillow for this purpose, and keeping a dream journal would all be helpful. You might also wish to formally ask the deity to visit your dreams, which can be done by saying the request aloud or saying it in front of your altar. A dream journal is a good idea regardless, since as you try some of the practices in this book the gods might appear in your dreams regardless of invitation. If the gods you are connecting with are associated with the Otherworlds or Faery, you may also find yourself wandering into those realms in your dreams as a biproduct of building a connection to those beings.

Journey Work

Journey work is the practice of entering a light trance state in order to send one's spirit or consciousness into the Otherworldly realm of the gods or other spiritual planes to seek knowledge, interact with, and connect with spiritual beings. It is something that can be engaged in ritualistically, such as creating a ceremony with the specific intention of contacting a deity, or it can be done as part of daily devotional. Any trace work, whether you are using a light trance or a deep one, requires practice and honing your mental skills. There is a great deal of material written about journey work and meditation skills. Reviewing techniques and adding to your skill set in this area will be invaluable to those who find journey work to be their primary vehicle for devotional connection.

Suggested Exercises

1. Take some time to discern what connecting to the divine feels like to you. Is it a feeling? A sound, smell, sensation? Spend some time journaling about it.

2. Create a daily devotional. Maybe it is a prayer, or something else entirely. Do your devotional for a week. Take notes if you can. Then after a week, reassess. What worked and what did not? When you created your devotional, did something sound better on paper but was difficult to do or say? After the first week, create a new devotional but make it a completely different style. Maybe your devotional for week one was a devotional dance, while the second week you can try quiet medita-

tion with a prayer you write. See how your experience changes. What worked better?

3. Find a picture or virtual tour of a sacred site that has meaning to you. Spend time studying the picture or re-watching the video tour of the sacred site. Print out a picture if you can. Take in the details. Spend some time doing journey work where you visit the site. What were your impressions? Did you encounter the deity connected to the site in your journey work or get other impressions from the spirit of that place? Journal your experiences.

CHAPTER THREE

Prayer

I have lovingly dubbed our destination today as Death Island. To travel to Death Island, we must travel across a choppy dark channel of ocean that separates the island from the rest of Ireland, in the Cable Car of Death. If you ever wish to travel to Dursey Island in the southwestern tip of the Beara Peninsula, the dwelling place of the god Donn and the place where the dead are thought to pass into the Otherworlds, then you will have to take a similar route. In a rickety old cable car that ferries you over to the island. The island itself is big enough to have a small town on it, and the ruins of a stone church. Visible from the western point of the island are three rocks, Bull Rock, Cow Rock, Calf Rock. Bull Rock or Tech Duinn is named for Donn and said to be where his body was interred. Donn is seen as a god of the dead and the underworld, and depending on your viewpoint, he is the first human to die in Ireland. He was a son of Mil, the people of the last invasion of Ireland who pushed the Irish gods into the faery hills. There are many versions of how he died. In one version as the sons of Mil approach the shores of Ireland there is a plague on their ship and Donn willingly sacrifices himself to the ocean so that his people may survive and make it to Ireland safely.

While we are on the island, we make offerings to Donn. I build a small cairn of palm-sized rocks near the ruins of an old stone church. I pour beer in offering on the ground, and I pray. Although I made light of our destination on our way here this morning, I feel the weight of Donn's presence here. Tech Duinn is quite impressive. There is a large cave like hole that bores through Bull Rock, and it indeed looks like an entrance to the underworld. I can see why people felt the dead passed into Donn's halls here in this place. My husband has just lost a close family member to cancer. Her death was not unexpected, but the blow of the loss is no less hard. He spends some quiet time offering prayers to Donn and saying good-bye to his beloved dead while he climbs to the highest point of the island. I have stayed closer to the cliffs, watching the ocean as it begins to drizzle lightly. I have my own prayers to offer Donn.

"Donn

Dark one

Keeper of the house of the dead

You who guard the entrance to the land of the ancestors

All must pass through your house

We honor you

We honor our ancestors

Blood and bone of those who have gone before

Ancestors of blood and ancestors of spirit

May our offerings honor you

May our offerings reach your house and bring succor to the dead

May we not fear to walk your realm when the times comes."

The rest of the prayer is less formal. I just spend time talking to Donn. My husband has lost someone; I on the other hand know I am about to lose someone. I don't know that anyone deals very well with such knowledge but I'm not dealing very well with it at all. My grandmother is dying. Slowly, inch by inch, from Alzheimer's. In many ways it is as if the woman who was the best part of my childhood is already dead. So much of who she is, is gone. So, I pray to the god of the dead, the god who takes the dead into his halls, to give her a swift transition. To ease her passage and give her rest. I sit there a long time, and I do feel a sense of peace and comfort from Donn. I feel the dead close by, not unsettled spirits, but ancestors at peace looking back towards the living.

Prayer has many purposes. It can bring comfort as it did to me on that faraway shore. It is also about placing trust in our gods, asking them to aid us in things that are beyond us. It is also a way for us to connect to the gods. Donn had not been a god I felt particularly close to. Yet his presence was very real and very vivid to me in that time, as I sat on his island offering him beer and tears and prayers. Prayer was my vehicle to contact him, and a solace in difficult times. When my grandmother did pass, I felt him there too, a comforting presence, reminding me my prayers were acknowledged and heard.

Prayer is not a word we hear often in Paganism. It took me a long time to realize I avoided using this word. Like "worship" it is another word that reminds many of the religions of their childhoods that they have rejected. While prayer is a concept that exists in all religions, we reject words and concepts that are significant in the religions we have become refugees from. Paganism seems so different from mainstream monotheism that we don't like to be reminded that some things are universal to all faiths.

Pagans do pray, we just call it something else. Most of the time we call them "invocations" and add lines like "Be here now!" or "We call you to this place!" to the end. When we remove those endings, what we are left with is essentially a prayer. Similarly, daily devotions usually include a prayer or mantra of some kind. But again, we avoid calling it by the dreaded "p" word.

So why pray? And what is a prayer anyway? What happens to us when we pray? Simply put, prayer is a way to commune and connect with the divine. You are reaching out to the infinite, and if it chooses, it can in turn reach out to you. When we pray, we step into sacred space, we set our thoughts and energy towards divinity. It opens us to communication with deity, and it also helps us build a relationship with deity. Prayer allows the gods to become familiar to us because it is a way to interact with them. It opens a dialogue. It can be verbal or non-verbal. If you have ever stood in front of your altar and spent a few minutes trying to connect to a deity, you have engaged in prayer. If you have ever praised a deity during ritual with the hopes that they would grace you with their presence, or help you in some way, you have engaged in prayer.

Prayer also allows us to reach out to a power that is higher than ourselves. We all want to think we are a magical badass, but we have our limits and we have limited sight. The gods can see where the threads of our actions cross with opportunity. They know the right timing for things, and which threads to pull to most effectively cause a desired outcome. I think as with most things there is power in asking the gods for anything. We have free will and I do think the gods influence some things, but for the most part we are left to clean up our own messes and gain our own rewards. If the gods influenced everything, we'd all be robots and have no real choices of our own. Prayer then can be a way to not only commune with the divine but ask for aid, to welcome their influence and power into our lives. If we don't ask, if we don't consent to some degree, the gods remain hands off in my opinion. This can also be true if your prayers are to the spirits of the land or the ancestors, or whatever power you are seeking to commune with. You have to ask; you have to start the conversation.

In general prayer can be divided into three categories: Petitions, Emulation, and Communion. Each follow a similar pattern but the purpose behind the prayers differs. Petition prayers revolve around asking for a specific thing from the gods. *"Help me find a better job." "Heal my child." "Protect my home from the hurricane."* These requests are usually specific and grounded in asking for something to happen in the physical world. Emulation prayer asks that we be bestowed with the same kind of qualities as the god we are calling upon. *"Brigid may my crafts be as fine as your own." "Thor may you fill me with your bravery."* You are asking that the traits the gods possess be present in yourself. Prayers of Communion concentrate on feeling the presence of the divine. These can also be prayers of thanks. You are not asking for anything other than being in the presence of divinity and feeling connected to them. This would be the kind of prayer work one would do as a daily devotion, where we ask that deity be present in our love throughout the day.

Creating Prayers

The biggest hurdle most Pagans have when they want to incorporate prayer into their devotional work is how to create them. Some books and certain traditions may have some prayers available. But Pagans worship such a wide range of beings from land spirits to gods, it's hard to find something specific to what you are praying to. If you grew up within a Christian structure, the dynamics of prayer aren't always explained. It's just a requirement. It's something you just do, and for the most part comes with premade sets of prayers. This can leave us at somewhat of a loss when choosing to follow a Pagan path. How does a Pagan pray? Well, for the most part, just like everyone else. Every region has some form of prayer and they have the same basic structures. Luckily, the Pagans of the past have left us several examples.

To find examples of Pagan prayer we can look to The Orphic Hymns to the Olympian Gods or Sigrdrífa's prayer in the *Sigrdrífumál*. Other prayers from the classical world can be found in Homer's *Iliad*. While in the Shinto region prayers are called *norito* and are intoned in a sing-song rhythmic pattern. These are all excellent examples to establish the pattern of prayer. Whether ancient or modern, prayers all have similar elements.

1. Call Out to the Gods/God/Spirit in Question
    a. Identify by name, titles, characteristics.
    b. Identify relationships, e.g. husband of ____, daughter of____ etc.
    c. Establish who you are talking to. Get their attention.
2. Praise How Awesome They Are
    a. You did all these great things. They are so cool and important.
    b. Butter them up and sing their praises.
3. State Agreements & Relationships Between You & Deity
    a. You have been my patron since _____.
    b. My mother, father, protector, guide.
    c. I am your priest/ess.

4. Requests, Petitions, or Thanking

    a. Grant me something.

    b. Help with something.

    c. May I embody your traits.

    d. Accept my thanks.

    e. Or all of the above.

The first part is basically dialing your area code. You are dialing your focus to a specific being or spirit. You are calling them by name, using their titles or naming their characteristics. By verbally naming and describing them there is no mistaking whose attention you are trying to get. Not unlike if someone calls your name in a crowded room, you will turn your head to see who called you, and in the same way you are getting the attention of the gods. The more descriptive you are, the better the picture you paint, the clearer the image in your mind. If you are saying a prayer publicly for a group, this also helps the others present to dial in their focus as well.

Step two is praising the being you are connecting to. In part it's a reminder of how powerful, how awesome and great they are. Don't be afraid to butter them up. The gods are awesome, and you probably wouldn't be trying to contact them if they weren't. This can work for land spirits, ancestors, or other spirits as well. Praising someone you are potentially asking something of is also never a bad idea.

Step three is to name any relationships or agreements between you and the gods. Why should they listen to you? Maybe you did them a favor or did a deed in their name, maybe you are a priest of this deity. Or it can be something as simple as acknowledging that you see them as a spiritual mother, father, etc. If you are calling to your ancestors, naming the family relationship is another element in dialing in your spiritual address and making sure you are connecting to the correct being. This is less about saying you *must* listen to me because I'm your priest, descendant, etc. and is more about establishing there is a connection between you and the being in question. Just because you have that connection doesn't mean you are owed gifts or aid from the gods, so it is important to make sure it is done respectfully. For example, some people avoid calling a deity mother/father because to some that implies that deity is obligated to offer aid, much like a mortal parent is obligated to aid a child. So, depending on the tradition you are part of and your views on deity this may or may not be appropriate. However you express the connection between yourself and deity, it is important that it is honest and done respectfully. At times this step is skipped depending on the person saying the prayer. Maybe you don't know the deity you are praying to yet and praying to seek a connection, in which case this might become a feature of future prayers when a clear relationship is established.

Step four would be naming the purpose for the prayer. Are you giving thanks to the gods? For something specific or perhaps being thankful for their presence in your life? Are you asking for something? Name whatever that specific task is. Or perhaps you seek to be imbued with the divine talents or attributes that deity possesses.

The order doesn't particularly matter. Although in most cases prayers will start with step one, naming the deity, and the rest can tend to appear in no particular order. Some prayers are meant to be sung or have a specific rhythmic nature. These elements usually vary with the language spoken or preferences and imagination of the one speaking it. That your prayer is heartfelt and has meaning to you is more important than trying to make something rhyme, etc.

Now that we know the building blocks of prayer, let us look at how they play out in some ancient examples of prayer.

This prayer from the *Sigrdrífumál* is spoken by the valkyrie Sigrdrífa (also known as Brynhildr) upon awakening from a magical sleep. Day here is thought to mean the goddess of the sun although she is not specifically named other than by her descriptive titles.

Hail, day! *Hail, sons of day!* *And night and her daughter now!*	Step 1. Here Sunna is not named specifically. Instead a description is used, and it is assumed to be understood.
Look on us here *with loving eyes,* *That waiting we victory win.*	Step 4. Petition, asking for the gods to look kindly on them and bring victory.
Hail to the gods! *Ye goddesses, hail,*	Step 1. Additional gods are praised, although not named.
And all the generous earth!	Step 2. Qualities of the goodness of the gods is named.
Give to us and goodly speech, *And healing hands, life-long.**	Step 4. Petition for wisdom, and asking that we emulate the qualities of the gods.
* Henry Adams Bellows, *The Poetic Edda* (Princeton: Princeton University Press, 1936), 389–390	

In the *Iliad* we find another example of prayer. Diomedes lets out a war cry and then prays to Athena to aid him. Afterwards we are told that Athena granted new-found strength into his arms and limbs, and in the stanza after Athena replies directly to the prayer telling him to take courage and that she will aid him. This prayer has all four of the elements of prayer. I also find it interesting that Athena replies, showing there was some expectation in the mind of ancient Pagans that it wasn't just a one-way conversation.

Hear me, Athena, unwearied daughter of aegis-bearing Zeus.	This one covers two steps at the same time. Step 1. Name of deity is given, her relation to other gods in the Pantheon, and a title. Step 2. She is praised, her unwearied quality is mentioned and praised.
If you've ever loved my father, stood by his side in murderous combat, be my friend now.	Step 3. Diomedes reminds Athena that his father is a favorite of hers, his family and the goddess have history, she has helped his family before and should do so again.
*Grant that I kill this man, that I come a spear's throw from the one who hit me unexpectedly and now boasts about it, saying I won't see daylight for much longer.**	Step 4. Asks for something. That he successfully slays his enemy.

* Homer, trans., Charles Stuart Calverley, *Homer's Iliad The Iliad of Homer, Volume 1* (University of Virginia: G. Bell, 1909), verses 110–120

Now that we have looked at prayers ancient people have written, let's look at a modern example written by a modern devotee. In this case one written in honor of the Irish god Lugh by Autumn Blackwood. I have intentionally not chosen one of my own prayers. I already know the steps. I intentionally use these steps when creating prayers. So, it wouldn't really illustrate the point that most, if not all prayers, have all these elements, even when the creator is not consciously aware of what the elements are. As with the other prayers, the steps can be mixed throughout the text of the prayer.

Lugh, you are goodness	Step 1. Deity is identified by name.
I pray for a long life. *I pray for your loving gaze.* *I pray for strong lungs* *for good speech* *I pray for Your strength to* *help carry me through a long life.* *I pray for a life* *with You.* *I pray for a people worth fighting for.* *For passion to fight for them*	Step 4. Petitioning deity for aid and blessings. Step 2. The qualities being petitioned for are qualities of deity being praised. Lugh is strong, so strength is asked for, he fought for a worthy noble people. Although they are framed as requests, they also reflect qualities the deity is being praised for possessing.

as you fought for the Tuatha, *the people of your birth though* *You were not raised among them.*	Step 1. The tribe of the deity is named, zeroing in on who exactly he is. There is a Welsh version of this deity as well, so this clarifies which Lugh we are calling upon. An aspect of his mythology is referred to, that he wasn't raised among the Tuatha. Step 2. His great deeds are described, fighting for the Tuatha.
I pray to be a recipient of a *fraction of that Loyalty.*	Step 4. The petition is continued, asking for a quality the deity possesses.

Ahead of me, you stand.	Step 3. No formal relationship is mentioned in the prayer, and this is often the step that may not necessarily appear in a prayer meant to be used by many different people for the same purposes. But this does establish a relationship; Lugh stands with the person offering the prayer. Lugh is at their side. It identifies the dynamic between the deity and the devotee.
*Lead me ahead. Lead me to You.**	Step 4. A continuation of the petition.

* Prayer created by Autumn Blackwood, used with permission. To find out more about Autumn and their devotional services check out their website: http://untamedpriestess.com/.

Other Kinds of Prayer

Not all prayer needs to have a set format or structure. When we are desperate or overcome with strong emotions, simply speaking from the heart is more than enough for prayer to be meaningful. If you are familiar enough with a god's energy and work with them often, you can make that connection to them non-verbally by thinking about them and your experiences with them. Prayer can also be sitting in front of your altar and just chatting with deity. For those who work with the ancestors, this is a good way to keep a strong connection with them. If they are someone you know in life, you are already familiar with chatting with them. You can see it as a chat to catch up with them, like you would someone you haven't seen in a long time. Tell them about what is happening in your life, tell them how much they meant to you or how much you miss them. For some, actions and movement can be more expressive than words. Prayer can be dance or movement. Don't be afraid to involve the rest of our body and not just your vocal cords.

Who are We Talking To?

In most of this book, I have used the term god/dess, deity, or divine in relation to prayer. But it is fair to note that these terms can be interchanged with others. Gods aren't the only beings we can commune with through prayer. The spirits of the land, the ancestors, angels, and the sidhe are all legitimate beings we can build a relationship with using prayer. As we have already discussed "deity" is a very loose term that different people and cultures have different ideas about. I suggest that you try to expand your ideas about the types of beings you can connect to through this practice. If you have only ever prayed to deity, go outside, take a little time communing with the land. Write a prayer for the spirit of the land you live on. It can become a routine practice to use your prayer to commune with the spirits where you live. You may be surprised by the results.

Not a One-Way Conversation

Although I do believe many Christians believe their god speaks to them in various ways, in general if we grew up being taught prayer within the lens of Christianity there isn't much expectation of a response. Perhaps that is part of the lack of appeal to converted Pagans. No one wants to sit there and think they are just talking to themselves. In my own experience prayer has always been a two-way conversation. How that conversation plays out is up to you. Maybe you have trouble hearing the voices of the gods clearly; instead you might get the sense that they are listening or that they are present around you. If you are praying for guidance you might receive a sign that has relevance to your prayer. Or you might simply keep running into symbols for that deity in unlikely places. The gods can speak to us in many different ways. You might hear clear messages, see imagery in your mind's eye, or just feel a comforting presence.

The Line Between Spell & Prayer

Within Pagan circles what I am usually asked when the topic of prayer comes up is, where is the line between magic and prayer? Both, in most cases, are an effort to effect change. If you pray for a new job, your end goal is aid in finding a new job. Prayer is all about belief and trust. There is no guarantee you will get what you are asking for. You have to believe both that a higher power is hearing your petition and that they have the ability to grant your request. You are essentially leaving the matter in their hands with the belief that they will know the right actions to take to grant it. It doesn't mean you don't put your own energy into it; certainly prayers where your energy has a clear focus have a better chance of bringing you what you are asking for. And there is certainly a clear exchange of energy in any prayer work, even when the purpose is simply to give thanks. We give so that we may receive. But the catch is there is no guarantee of return. You can't be that friend who gives someone a gift only to expect a favor be done because of your generosity. Prayers aren't buying off the gods.

If you attack a problem magically you are essentially the director of the energy. You are writing the code, describing what should manifest, how and when, etc. This is limited by your information about the problem. You may not know all the factors in the situation or be able to see all the opportunities, or maybe you didn't get the timing right. When we petition the gods there is no guarantee of results. We are not making demands after all, we are asking. But it comes with the benefit that they have better information to work with and they are the ones holding the reins. They have a greater amount of influence in the world than we do. Magic that includes calling on the gods, or theurgy, blends the concept of magic and prayer, but I think too often in this practice we don't really give up the control to the gods. We instead have a specific vision of what we want to manifest to be the end result. Maybe there is a better outcome that is possible, maybe we think it's what we want but it will end badly, or we limit ourselves to a very narrow image of what we want and often won't get great results. In magic you are the one weaving the threads, while in prayer the gods are the ones weaving the thread of manifestation and fate together.

Let me tell you a story. A story about a prayer to Hekate. You can decide if the line between magic and prayer were blurred, and if it matters or not. Not that long ago I was scrolling through Facebook and came across an article about a college student in New York whose dog, Theo, was stolen. She tied him up outside a grocery store that the two were regulars at and while in the store someone stole the little dog. Video surveillance from the store caught a man yanking the poor elderly dog abusively on his harness. The story was blasted all over the internet and on the news. The young woman offered a reward for the return of the dog, and a promise to not press charges. All she wanted was her dog back. The dog also had health issues that required medication, so that was also a concern. The surveillance pictures of this poor little dog being swung around by his leash like an unimportant object by the thief were horrifying. All I could think was how devastated I would feel if someone stole my animals, and what I would do to get them back. I'm also not stupid and grew up in New York. Someone stealing pets, small docile pets, is likely planning on using them as a bait dog used in dogfighting, and that was an even more horrifying thought. All day I couldn't get the image of that little dog being taken out of my mind. I couldn't stop thinking how I would have felt, and how unfair it was. So, I went before my altar to Hekate, I made offerings, I prayed to her for the safe return of the dog. I knew there was a small chance if any that someone hadn't already abused this animal, but I prayed anyway. I asked that someone watching the news might want to get the reward or feel guilt, whatever made them turn the dog in. I sent up my feelings of sorrow and fury to Hekate and I prayed that she bring the dog home safely, that she could find a way to bring justice if nothing else.

It was intense, there was a lot of energy and emotion there. It was a weaving of offerings, words and will, that ultimately, I handed over to her to do with as she saw fit. I trusted her to hunt and find, to bring justice, to do what I frankly could not.

I understand that in both magic and prayer belief is important. Just like in magic if you really believe your spell won't work, well, it won't. If your focus is on magic not working, you make it not work. I also knew the chances of getting the dog, probably used as a bait dog, back where probably almost nothing. I kept my mind blank of those thoughts and let my faith rest in that Hekate would do whatever she could, be that save the dog or justice. And I knew her ability to enact justice was very, very high. Something would happen. Even if I never knew what that something was. And that was good enough for me. Something was better than nothing.

Two days later, on a whim, I looked up the story again to see if there was any follow-up. I was happy to find that beyond all hope a woman did see the news report and called in to return the dog for the reward. The college student was overjoyed to have her dog back. I was astonished and incredibly happy. Granted other people were offering their thoughts and prayer too, I wasn't the only one. And I like to think that collective asking of the divine for aid helped. I immediately went to my altar again and made offerings and offered prayers of thanks to Hekate.

Prayers aren't just for ourselves; it isn't just about getting the things we want and need. Sometimes it's about asking the divine to help others and taking joy in seeing your prayers answered. Did being a Witch and knowing how to focus my will and energy help? I'm betting it did. Quite often I approach prayer and magic in similar ways. Perhaps there were elements of magic that overlapped in what I did. But I think there was a fundamental difference. I came to the table wanting a specific thing, just as I would if I was tackling the problem from a purely magical angle. Energy was raised, sure. But Hekate was the one who wove it all together. While if I was going the spellwork route, I would be doing that part and forcing my will upon the fabric of the universe. In a way it all comes down to faith. She wasn't obligated to help me, yet I had faith that she would. Faith, belief, trust, whatever you want to call it, I believed that she would be able to see and find the things I could not, that she could make the biggest difference. I could have done a spell and just used my will and energy; maybe it would have been the same result, maybe not. There is a humbling element to prayer. It requires that you acknowledge that you aren't always the most powerful thing out there. It requires that you have faith in the beings that you trust your needs and desires with to be more powerful and benevolent. I think if I had attacked the problem purely magically, the results wouldn't have been the same, but then again that's because I have a great deal of faith in Hekate. And prayer can't function without faith of some kind.

Suggested Exercises

1. Write a prayer. Use the format given to create something for whatever deity or being you feel close to. The more comfortable you become with the process, the easier it will become to create your own prayers.

2. Build a prayer practice. This isn't something that will happen overnight. It should be an organic process; the only requirement is that you keep consistently doing it.

Spend some time deciding where you want to incorporate prayer into your spiritual practice. Is it a daily prayer you say by your altar? Is it something you will say on a specific day to honor a particular being?

3. Build a practice of gratitude. Most of the time prayer isn't about getting something. Or at least it shouldn't be. Be grateful for the things you do have, for the presence of the divine in your life. Create a prayer that focuses on gratitude. Try using it every day for a week.

4. Journal about your experiences. I know, I know, the dreaded journaling. But it is worthwhile. Journal about how you feel when you pray. What kinds of prayers are you creating? What kind of response are you getting from deity? After a month go back and see how your practice has evolved or changed. Then in another few months look back again and see how your practice has evolved and grown.

CHAPTER FOUR

Offerings

I stand near the docks, the smell of salt and sea water swirling around me, as I say the prayer softly.

> *"Mannan Mac Lir*
> *God of the waves*
> *To you the waves of the ocean are as solid land is to us*
> *The white crested waves are your horses*
> *We greet you as we travel out on the water that covers*
>   *your realm*
> *We seek the blessing of your wisdom and presence*
> *May we travel safely through your realm and back again."*

It is a surprisingly sunny day by Irish standards. The sailors are quite pleased by it and in a good mood. They speculate we will be able to stay out on the water for our whale watch for longer than expected. They deliver on that promise, keeping us out most of the day. As I get on the small boat with the rest of the pilgrims who are joining us on this tour of southern Ireland, I clutch a small palm-sized bag. We are going out onto the ocean to seek more than just the whales the boat tour advertises. We seek to connect to Mannan Mac Lir, the Irish god of the sea and magic, and who has a bit of a reputation as a trickster. In the small bag I have several offerings for him. Some fresh-picked flowers, several herbs, a small stone, and a small shell from a childhood summer trip to the beach. Each have a meaning to me. I realize how much I miss the ocean as I breathe in the sea air. The air that fills my lungs is exhilarating and cleansing, the sound of the waves crashing is soothing. I used to live only a few miles from the ocean growing up, but it has been a long time since I have been able to visit the water as often as I did in childhood. Although all the oceans technically belong to Mannan, it feels right to offer him a shell from my side of the ocean to the waters here in his realm near the shores of Ireland.

We are all excited as we get on the water. There are no clouds and the sun reflecting on the water makes everything look dazzling and beautiful. We take pictures and chat, then the boat stops, and the motor cuts off. We bob more heavily in the water and our guides tell us if we are lucky, we might see some dolphins or minke whales. Our guides also point out different landmarks along the shore. No whales appear so after a little bit we move onward. Second stop still no whales. The third time we stop I take a moment alone to scatter the contents of my offering bag into the waters. I watch as the small shell sinks below the waves; the herbs and flowers remain floating on the surface. As I watch the herbs floating a head bobs up out of the water, a seal that looks curiously at us. I hear others exclaiming that they see other seals too. They follow alongside the boat for a few minutes. I take it as a good sign and smile. That is when the whales start breaking the *surface, and I feel Mannan's presence there with us. I silently send my gratitude to him for letting us see the creatures of his realm, feeling filled with his presence and the simple joy of experiencing the beauty of this place. There are many times I have made offerings to the gods. I think then that perhaps it is too often when I need their aid, but I find that sometimes it is the offerings I make in gratitude, in reverence and awe of the gods that I find the most meaning in and find the most connection with them in.*

In HBO's series *Rome* there is a scene where one of the main characters is imprisoned. Things aren't looking good; he is sitting in dirt and filth and he is desperate for aid. He doesn't have anything fine to offer the gods as he prays fervently; all he has is a small bug that he smashes with his fist as an offering. Another character is soon after seen making a proper offering of a bull in a temple; her prayers are not as sincere. Ironically, things don't go so well for her. Yet the character who prays with all his being who offers the gods literally the only thing he has, a meager insect, is shown their favor and escapes his imprisonment. This has always struck me as a quintessential example of what an offering is. So much of what goes into an offering is the energy you put behind it. Sometimes a fine offering is appropriate, even essential, and sometimes your most heartfelt prayers might be accompanied by a very meager offer that is simply all that you have at the time.

I wasn't exposed to the concept of making offerings before I entered Paganism. There was a bit of a learning curve and I tried to figure out what to offer and how to make offerings. It seemed so confusing. Sometimes the kind of item offered was important; other times the gods asked me to offer them things I felt weren't of enough value. Ultimately the choices I made about my offerings were on a case-by-case basis. Some things were guided by research; other things relied heavily on what my connection to deity told me.

Simply put, offerings are gifts. Gifts we give to gods and spirits. It is a practice that spans religions and time. Historical and archeological records show us it was a vital part of the religious worship of ancient peoples. Items offered to the gods vary greatly from livestock, artfully crafted jewelry or weapons, wine and liquor, to music and dance. The types of things offered to the gods varied greatly, but what remains consistent is that whatever was offered was something considered of great value to the person offering it. Value varies from person to person. To the farmer their cattle is their livelihood and is something of very high value. To the artist their art is more valuable in their eyes than a cow. Culturally what has value will depend on what that culture values. To the person dying of thirst in the desert the water in their canteen is more valuable than gold. Value can be a matter of perspective as well as culturally taught.

Just like with people, gifts are given for different reasons. We give gifts in celebrations, such as a birthday. We give gifts to thank people whom we appreciate or to show love. Sometimes we give gifts as peace offerings, such as a gift of flowers after an argument to make amends with a partner. Gifting to the gods is not much different; we make offerings to the gods for very similar reasons. But giving a gift to a nonphysical being can be tricky. There is no post office address for Zeus, so how do we get our offerings to the gods? In many cases ancient people felt that destroying an item, either breaking it or burning it, would transfer the essence of their gifts to the unseen realm of the gods. Exquisitely crafted weapons that have been ritualistically broken have been found in bogs in Germany, Denmark, and the British Isles. The Nydam ship is an Iron Age ship found ritually sunk in a bog in Denmark, presumably as a gift to the gods. The area also contains many caches of swords and other ritually destroyed items.

It is clear that ancient Pagans, no matter the culture you look at, understood that the gods were under no obligation to help them. They made offerings to the gods not just for things they wanted help with, but also to avoid calamity. If the gods were happy with you, recognized you, and saw how you honored them, then you were less likely to catch disease, have the crops fail, etc. To modern eyes this looks like bribery, in part because of how we have been taught to view the divine. Many Pagans, coming from being raised in Abrahamic religions, tend to view the gods as divine parents, parents that have an *obligation* to help their children. But assuming the gods are only there to serve us and must help us can be a dangerous point of view, and one that will probably lead to disappointment. That isn't to say the gods do not care about us, but they are gods; they also deserve awe and respect. Instead of seeing offerings as bribery we should think of offerings as a path to building right relationships with the spirits we worship. This would certainly be more in line with ancient views of the gods. Having a way to offer our thanks and gratitude when they do bestow us with gifts, and quite simply to be able to express our awe and devotion to them, is essential to forming that kind of relationship and remaining in right relation to the gods. All of which we can do through offerings.

What to Offer?

Offerings can quite literally be almost anything. They can be physical objects like incense, herbs, wine, liquor, milk, flowers, or pieces of art. Nonphysical things can also be offerings, such as singing a song, dancing, or a task that is completed by yourself in honor of a deity. Whether the being you are making the offering to will like or accept that offering will depend on the deity in question. This is where knowing your mythology and developing a strong connection to deity is important. The more you know about the deity, the easier selecting an offering will be.

Many times, a god might tell you what they want as an offering. Sometimes it is something you might not expect. Other times it might be something you never thought a deity would ask for. If it is something you cannot find, then it is ok to have a conversation with deity explaining the thing that is asked for isn't something you can offer at this time. But often the request is something you can fulfill; you just didn't think it is something they would want.

Value can be difficult to determine. The importance we place on items differs from person to person. Items given as offerings to the gods can be something you crafted by hand, putting your personal energy into. That could be anything from a drawing to a poem or a piece of jewelry. It could be a wine that you find exceptionally delicious, or herbs you gathered by hand that have specific meaning to you or have relevance to the deity you are offering them to. The possibilities are really endless. What you should not offer is food or wine that has spoiled, or things you don't deem to be of good value. For example, if I was offering a deity a cut of meat and I took the best cut and cooked it and ate it and only left the fat and gristle for my offering, essentially the parts I would throw away that aren't something of value, isn't very respectful. I am taking the best and giving to gods the insulting scraps. That is not going to go over very well.

It is Not about an Even Exchange

Most of the time we are the ones selecting the offerings we make, but sometimes the gods ask for specific things. Sometimes those requests can be just outright odd. What is important to keep in mind is that it's not about giving and getting equivalent things. Here is an example. My friend Bryan got a speeding ticket and here is the story of how he got out of that ticket, with some godly intervention. He asked Loki for help getting out of the ticket and Loki agreed, and asked my friend to buy him a cup of coffee as payment. My friend thought this was kind of silly. A cup of coffee wasn't an offering of high value; that was easy. But the response he felt Loki gave him was "Don't worry about it. How often does someone buy me coffee? Just buy me the cup of coffee and you'll see." So, he did, and when he went to try to fight the ticket, he did miraculously get out of it, quite easily. A cup of coffee might not be much to you or me, but getting someone out of a parking ticket probably isn't that hard for the god of mischief either. Many of the things we ask the gods for may seem unattainable to us but are easily within the reach of a god. There are times when offering something of great personal value is appropriate, but sometimes a $2 cup of coffee will do. There also may be times when you wish to make an offering when it is not possible to offer something elaborate.

Energy Exchange

Offerings helps us build a relationship of reciprocity with the gods; there is an exchange of energy, and a connection formed by doing so. Making regular offerings at an altar or particular place can also bring the presence of the gods closer into our lives. But our mindset when giving offerings is very important. Offerings are a way to give our gratitude and reverence to the gods as well as petition for aid. You should make offerings regularly and not just when you want something. That is akin to only calling one's parents when they need something. If there is no relationship there to begin with if you don't have a strong bond with deity beforehand then chances of receiving aid for something important are lower. Just because you made that offering to Brigid way back when on Beltane three years ago, doesn't mean she's under any obligation to listen to you now. Offerings helps us build a relationship of reciprocity with the gods and spirits. There is an exchange of energy, and a connection formed by doing so.

Giving to Receive vs. Gifting

It is important to keep in mind that making an offering isn't a bribe. It's a gift. It doesn't mean an instant return on what you are giving up, which may be why so many are reticent to offer the gods things of value. There is risk, and a handful of incense is safer than throwing a silver ring you have prized for many years into the fire. I think we all have experienced someone giving us a gift with strings attached, just so they can get something from us. That doesn't go over any better with the gods than it does with most people.

How Do I Know the Offering Was Accepted?

Just because we made an offering doesn't mean it is instantly accepted or liked. The problem could be in the item offered or the sincerity in which it is offered, among other factors. In general, when alcohol that is offered evaporates fairly quickly on the altar, I take it as a good sign. For example, if I left an offering the night before and in the morning most of it has vanished, which shouldn't happen overnight, I feel it has been accepted. On the opposite end of the spectrum if an offering has been made recently and you return to find it in a negative state, spoiled or the vessel it was offered in was broken, I would not view that as something that was accepted. For example, there was a period of time the goddess Brigid was trying to get my attention and I just wasn't making the time for her that I should have. I forgot to make offerings and my time was focused on other gods. Eventually I went to make a sort of apology offering of cream in a bowl on her altar. I gave you some nice cream, so you have to accept my apology, right? Wrong. Later that day I noticed a funky smell in the house. When I tracked it down, I realized it was the cream, which had somehow curdled in less than an hour. To add to that an army of ants was invading the altar to get to the funky now-solid cream. As far as I'm aware fresh-bought cream shouldn't turn into funky noxious goo within an hour. So, I took it as a sign I had more amends to do.

Another good go-to tool to determine if an offering has been accepted is to do divination. This doesn't need to be a full reading, but you can instead pull a single ogham, an oracles card, rune, etc. Based on the meaning of the divination method of your choice, you should be able to determine if the offering was acceptable.

Disposing of Offerings

Unless you burn your offering in a fire you will have physical remnants of your offerings to dispose of. I personally feel it is the energy of the item that we are offering to the gods, so after that item has been on the altar for a certain amount of time I feel it is ok to toss the offering. Many people refrain from tossing offered items in the garbage and prefer to bury them or leave them outside. This can be a special tree where you leave the remains of offerings on a regular basis, or you might choose to bury items. If you have burnt something down to ashes, you might way to dispose of the ashes by leaving them in a body of water. But if you dispose of offerings this way, you really have to consider the impact the item you are leaving out in nature can have on the environment. Could an animal eat this and be harmed or poisoned by it? Will this item negatively affect the environment or pollute it? If you think the answer is yes, then don't do it. I'd rather dispose of an item responsibly and toss it in the trash bin than bring it to a natural place and harm that place in the process. Again, it's the energy of the item that you have given; what's left is just the shell and is ok to dispose of, even if it's right into the trash bin.

The impact of offerings that were made with good intention but without much thought, can be seen at many sacred sites across the world. When visiting Ireland, I saw a variety of offerings at many sites that had basically turned into trash covering the site. In many cases the offerings were harming the monuments themselves. When I visited the Cailleach's stone on the Beara Peninsula our group spent most of our time at the site pulling out coins that had been wedged into crevasses in the rock. Some had rusted and were wearing away the stone, while others clearly had broken off weaker areas of the stone. Buttons, tea lights, and other items had also been jammed into any available crevasse. Removing these items felt like our offering to the Cailleach. Afterwards the site felt better, the energy moving instead of stagnant. Many of the sites we visited had donation boxes at the entrance to help with the upkeep of the site, and we deposited the coins we had taken from the Cailleach's stone in the box at the next site we visited. At other sites we saw coins that had been jammed into living trees, many of which the bark has started to grow over, but the sheer number of them in the trees were obviously not healthy for the tree. Just because other people are doing it, or it's part of a tradition, doesn't mean we are excused from considering the impact our offerings can have on the environment. We are making an offering out of love and respect to the gods; those gifts shouldn't be something that harms the world around us.

Timing & Protocols

Depending on the deity there may be a certain time when offerings are made. For example, historically the Greeks had a cycle of specific times religious observations were held based on the moon phase during the month. A meal was offered to Hekate and the restless dead on the new moon, while other moon phases were important to other gods in the pantheon. If you are a devotee of Hekate then this is important information and may influence when you make offerings to her.

In other traditions there may be specific items that can be offered to a deity, and some that should never be offered and are considered offensive. This will vary depending on the culture and traditions surrounding that deity. Knowing what these do's and don'ts are requires research on the devotee's part. Learn about the culture and customs surrounding that deity, both ancient and modern. While I feel the gods are forgiving to a degree, knowing about a taboo before you commit it is safer in the long run. When gods and spirits are used to receiving certain items or used to having certain protocols observing when those offerings are given to them over long periods of time, not observing these protocols can be viewed as disrespectful.

When You Have Nothing to Offer

There will be times when you feel an offering is appropriate, but you don't have anything on hand. On one such occasion I ended up in the hospital for an ear infection that caused massive vertigo. I had been traveling for an event, and traveling in an airplane had made the situation worse. The event was outdoors, there was no AC, and it was a summer with record-breaking heat. So, on top of my ear infections I had managed to make myself severely dehydrated as well. At one point it felt like hours before I could open my eyes and tell which way was up and which way was down. It was horrible, and I still had to travel on another flight to get home. At one point when I was using the bathroom in my hospital room, I brought a small cardboard juice carton I had been given with my hospital lunch. I poured it down the drain and spoke a heartfelt prayer to Brigid to help me recover. Things did go better after that. A juice box isn't exactly an offering of high value, but it was literally all I could get my hands on and the energy behind my offering and prayers were heartfelt. Brigid seemed to find it worthy and that was what mattered.

Offering Bodily Fluids

There are many, myself included, who do offer a few drops of their own blood as an offering on occasion. Whether you use this type of offering will depend on your comfort level, the deity or spirit it is offered to, and your tradition. In Santeria the spirits are fed by blood, specifically from animals that are eaten by the community afterwards in most cases. Using my own blood as an offering in my mind would not be appropriate to a deity that regularly receives offerings of this nature from things viewed as food. I'm not offering myself as food. To other deities there may not be this connotation and it can be appropriate, but it is not, like many things, something that is universal.

One should also not view blood as simply another ingredient. When you offer your own blood, you are offering a piece of your-self, your life force, your essence and energy. You can charge your blood to fuel a certain purpose or carry your gratitude to the gods as well. You are also offering something that was handed down by your ancestors and holds the memory of countless lifetimes besides your own. It can be a very sacred and meaningful offering.

Health and safety concerns should also be taken into consider-ation. For myself this kind of offering is a private one, one that I might offer before going to a ritual or during a personal rite with-out others present. This eliminates issues of transmitting disease. Using lancets, which can easily be found in a pharmacy, would also be beneficial sanitation and avoid harming oneself by mistake.

Blood is certainly not the only bodily fluid that can be offered, but again the same concerns over health and disease transmission and if it is appropriate to the deity should be considered.

Forgetting to Give Offerings

It is important to consider that a great many beings are fairly used to being given offerings. Depending on the culture it may even be seen as rude to not do so when contacting a particular being. Other blunders we can create for ourselves. For example, there was a weekend event where I was hosting a ritual, where I accidently forgot to make an offering to the sidhe. The temple space we had created had a number of gods honored in it, and we also had a separate area for the sidhe as well. Everyone was assigned a deity to give an offering to and say a prayer to at the public opening of the space for the weekend. There was a person who spoke a poem to honor the sidhe, but an offering was not poured as there had been for the other gods. It was something that none of us noticed at the time. It had also been raining badly and we had been forced to move the temple space to a dryer location, so we were all a bit frazzled. Fast-forward to a few hours later when we were preparing for ritual. Part of the ritual required that it be a darker setting, so we had decided to start just at nightfall and have tiki torches around the space. Only problem was no one could find the tiki torches. I looked everywhere. I thought I knew where I'd left them, but they were not there. I tore apart our cabin, our car, everywhere I could think of and no torches. Finally, I gave up and we had to make do for the ritual with other light sources. Afterwards a few of us walked into the main hall of the campground we were using for the event and right there in plain sight were all the tiki torches and the giant bottle of fluid I had been searching for. Only I had walked past the table they were on in my mad search for them at least a dozen times. We all thought about it and then realized our blunder. The sidhe hadn't been given an offering or libation as the other gods had. Sure, they had something said for them, the gods had as well, but we had slighted them by not also giving an offering. We also considered that in past years we had given them a physical offering of milk, butter, etc. This had been the only time we hadn't. We had just kind of forgotten. So, they had taken our stuff. We immediately sent someone to the grocery store a few miles away from the camp to buy heavy cream for them. In somewhat of a panic we searched the camp to see what else we could offer to make amends and promptly brought a giant slice of cake to the temple and offered it to them along with the cream. The sidhe were given a great many more offerings that weekend, intentionally giving them extra as an apology and peace offering for our blunder. Nothing else went missing and the rain even stopped, and we had nice weather the rest of the weekend.

In other cases, you might simply forget to make your regular offerings to deity. Life gets in the way sometimes. Personally, I tend to try to make amends by making additional offerings or asking what you can do to right the situation if you feel the being in question is upset about regular offerings suddenly stopping, or if an offering that has been consistently given at a certain time is not given.

Steps for Identifying Appropriate Offerings

When it comes to making offerings, even when you are aware of items often given to a deity, it is important to use some critical thinking to break down why you are choosing to give an offering. In general, there are six steps to determining whether or not an offering is appropriate. We will look at these steps in detail, then we will look at them broken down in relation to deities I personally worship. I encourage you to use this chart for your own deities. Even when you have a long-standing practice, breaking down each element can help you in the future to refine your practices and add to them. You can't add to a practice if you haven't examined why you are engaging in it in the first place.

Step 1. What Is the Context?

This is important because different circumstances will likely set you in different directions for your offerings. For example, if I was making an offering in relation to doing healing work my offering would be very different than if I was making an offering in hopes of receiving aid connected to finances. Even if the offering was given to the same deity, the reasons behind the offering changes what I offer.

Step 2. What Does Mythology/Folklore Tell Us?

This requires some research. It doesn't mean that you have to comb through every known myth about a deity. You should eventually try to be as well read as possible in the myth of a deity you worship. But if you are just starting out on your journey with a deity, you also aren't expected to know everything. This could mean you might reach out to someone who does know that deity's mythology very well for some help. In general, it helps to focus on one myth at a time, especially if the deity has many aspects or areas of dominion. Read through the myth and see what resonates with you about that story. Look for items, traits, actions, food, drinks, and places that are mentioned or connected to what happens in the story. Also note if these things are items/qualities that the deity likes or dislikes.

Step 3. What Was Offered Historically?

This information may or may not be available to you. In many cases we don't know what items were historically offered to certain deities. That's ok, if there isn't any information about historical offerings then this step won't play into what you decide to offer. You may find only information about specific times offerings were made, which can be useful. There is also the possibility that the kind of historical offerings that were made are inappropriate or repugnant to a modern person. Just because something was offered historically doesn't always mean it is appropriate today. If that is the case, try to look at the reasons ancient people might have offered these items. What was the reason behind their choice? A cultural belief? Something relating to the region in which they lived? Then consider if you can come up with an appropriate offering that resonates with those reasons.

Step 4. What Does the Deity Say?

It is entirely possible to offer something culturally and historically valid and get absolutely no response from deity. Not all offerings have to be based on what other people have offered in the present or past. Many times, the deity will tell you what they want, you just have to ask. Spend some time meditating and reaching out your awareness to the deity. Either out load or in your mind, state your intention to be open to receiving information from them. Ask them what they wish to be given as an offering. You can get into details here as well. Ask them how long they wish this to be an offering that you will give them. When and how often should it be given?

Step 5. Availability & Safety

In some cases, the items given to deity historically, connected to their myths, or even ones they have relayed they wish to have given to them, are not within your means to give. It might be an item you can not afford to buy. It could be something illegal or inappropriate. There are deities that in the past were offered human sacrifices after all, that doesn't mean I as a modern person should do the same. Other offerings may not be safe for a variety of reasons. At an event I organize we stopped burning stick and coal incense in our temple space because there were a few people in the group who had asthma and allergies that made going into the temple space and breathing in the smoke hazardous to them. Instead we used an oil diffuser (specifically with scents that didn't bother their allergies) and fresh flowers to bring in the element of scent to the space as an offering to deity.

Step 6. Divination to Verify

Once we have determined what we are going to offer, it is important to verify we are on the right path. This could be pulling cards, runes, ogham, mediumship, or whatever system you personally use to determine if the deity is happy with the choice. This can be done before making the offering. In larger group workings I have used it afterwards as well to determine if the offering was accepted. It can also help you determine if you need to change anything.

Next, we will look at these steps in relation to items I offer to the Morrigan, Dagda, Bast, Hekate, and Freya. The items listed for each for the purposes of these examples are only some of many offerings I give to these deities. It is also important to take into consideration that another devotee of these same deities may use these same steps and come up with a completely different item with their own justifications for its use. In many ways this is the entire point. An item should be meaningful, but also have meaning that you can personally identify with. If you asked two devotees of the same deity to write a list of five different offerings they give to that deity, more than likely there would be some similarities. Yet if you try this experiment you will inevitably have at least one or maybe two items that are different. So, my list isn't going to be the same as yours, not even for the same gods, and it isn't supposed to be. Mimicking someone's version of devotion can only get you so far. You have to discover what your devotion looks like. Which means what others do are just guideposts for you along the way. In many ways this is why I prefer breaking down the steps for you in many of these areas of devotion. Giving you the steps helps you discover your own answers. Keeping all that in mind, here is my own breakdown for creating offerings to these powerful deities.

Deity	Offering Chosen	Step 1. What Is the Context?	Step 2. What Does Mythology/Folklore Tell Us?	Step 3. What Was Offered Historically?
Morrigan	Milk	An offering when asking for blessings.	She tricks Cuchulainn into healing her wounds when she appears to him in disguise and he asks for a drink of milk from her cow.	No records survive.
Dagda	Oak cask aged beer	An offering during a Samhain ritual.	The Dagda is connected to the oak tree. Splits in an oak trunk are said to be made by the Dagda's axe, and one of the names for his magical harp is "Oak of Two Meadows"	No records survive.

Deity	Offering Chosen	Step 1. What Is the Context?	Step 2. What Does Mythology/Folklore Tell Us?	Step 3. What Was Offered Historically?
Hekate	A large decorative key that I etched her epithets on	An offering for a ritual to protect the home.	I looked to her historical and documented titles. Hekate is connected to keys, her epithet "Kleidouchos" means "key bearer." I carved this and two other epithets related to protection in some way on the key. "Alexeatis" meaning "Averter of Evil" and "Amaimaketos" meaning "Unconquerable" or "Invincible."	Keys don't seem to have been a historical offering, although they are one of her symbols. There are several historical sources that mention offerings to Hekate such as the *Argonautica* by Apollonius of Rhodes and Ovid's "Metamorphoses". These include garlic, honey, sheep, dogs, wine, milk, frankincense, cakes, or wafers. The animal sacrifices are not appropriate for my personal modern practice. There are some cultures that still offer food animals as ritual offerings, but I am not trained in doing such, and it doesn't fit my personal ethos. Although the carved key is my primary offering, the food items such as honey and garlic are items I can offer alongside my key offering.

Deity	Offering Chosen	Step 1. What Is the Context?	Step 2. What Does Mythology/Folklore Tell Us?	Step 3. What Was Offered Historically?
Bast	Perfume with frankincense and myrrh	Offerings given during daily devotions.	One of her titles was "Lady of Perfume."	Votive offerings of bronze cat statues, mummified cats. Mummified cats are not something I consider appropriate for myself as a modern worshiper and doesn't really fit what I am looking to do. There are already a few small votive cat statues on her altar, so that doesn't really change my course of action either.
Freya	Honey	An offering of welcoming, to be given before journey work when I first was connecting with Freya.	Freya cries tears of gold and is connected to gold in general. She is also connected to sex and pleasure among other things. Honey is sweet and enjoyable to eat and it is also gold in color, so this connection to gold is why I chose this offering.	There is some historical evidence of rings and other gold items being thrown into springs or bodies of water, but there isn't any clear indication they were offered specifically to Freya. This doesn't necessarily help me with this particular offering as I am making the offering at an indoor altar.

Deity	Step 4. What Does the Deity Say?	Step 5. Availability & Safety	Step 6. Divination to Verify
Morrigan	When meditating on what to offer, the imagery of the story of Cuchulainn and the Morrigan healing one another came to mind and felt important in relation to the offering.	Easily available from the grocery store. I am not lactose intolerant, so this is a safe offering for myself.	I drew three oracle cards to verify I was on the right track. The cards pulled where Blessings, Cattle, and Cuchulainn. I took this a positive verification.
Dagda	After a short meditation where I asked what he wanted, I was given the clear image that he wanted beer. When I asked what kind, he indicated I should peruse the liquor store and I would know which one.	Easily available from a local liquor store. In the ritual it was poured in an offering bowl. After the ritual it was poured on a ritual fire so there was no harm to anything in the surrounding area from the offering in any way.	When I walked into the liquor store, right in front there was a display advertising an oak-aged microbrewery creation. This fit the mythology and the directions he gave me. This in itself can be seen as a sign of verification, but I also pulled a card to verify once I got home that this is what he wanted.

Deity	Step 4. What Does the Deity Say?	Step 5. Availability & Safety	Step 6. Divination to Verify
Hekate	I spend time connecting to Hekate and while the item she wishes offered to her isn't specified I do get clear direction on where on our property she wishes me to bury the offering and that I must do so after dark on a new moon.	I verify what the decorative key is made of to make sure it will not be toxic to anything in the yard, animals or plants, once I bury it.	I don't pull cards for this one; instead I spend time at Hekate's altar offering her incense and meditating to confirm the key offerings and the way I will be offering it is acceptable, or if she wants me to do something additional.
Bast	While making a different kind of offering to Bast, I reached out mentally to confirm that the offering was accepted. It was but I got the sense that she was saying, "This is nice, but I want this next time." In my mind I got the sense of sweet rich smells that uplifted and filled the senses.	I personally don't have any allergies to any perfumes. I made sure I selected something that would not be harmful to the animals in the house and made sure the statue of Bast I planned on anointing with the perfume was sealed so it would not harm the statue.	After selecting three perfumes I personally liked, I pulled a card for each to see which would be most favorable to Bast.

Deity	Step 4. What Does the Deity Say?	Step 5. Availability & Safety	Step 6. Divination to Verify
Freya	At the point I started making this offering I was just beginning to connect to Freya, so I wasn't really getting much information directly from her. I simply felt her presence and wasn't getting an indication one way or another if this is what she wanted. You will not always get a strong response from deity until after making several offerings and after building a stronger connection to them.	Easily available at the grocery store. My cat enjoys trying to steal this offering and since sugar isn't good for cats, I make sure the door to the room with this altar is closed when I make this offering. I make sure the offering is disposed of respectfully outside where the cat cannot get it.	I end my journey work with a prayer to Freya that ends with the line "May this offering be accepted." Afterwards I spend a few quiet moments letting myself be open to whatever Freya wishes to impart to me, and energetically feel if the offering feels accepted.

Suggested Exercises

1. Pick a myth about the deity you feel connected to and spend time studying it. Think about the qualities of the deity described in the myth. What themes and qualities are emphasized? Is there a specific item, herb, object, deed that is done or offered in connection to the deity? Use the information you gather to create a meaningful offering. For example, if healing is an element of the myth find an herb that is known for its healing qualities that is local to where you live. Use the herb as an offering to the deity. Record your results in your journal.

2. Spend time opening your awareness to the deity. Ask them what they want you to offer them. Record your impressions in your journal. Try this throughout the year, and see if what the deity asks for changes. Are different things requested during different parts of the year? Or when you are going through different situations in your life?

3. Create a schedule that you can stick to for making offerings to the deity. If it is one day a week, stick to it for at least a month. Record your impression in your journal. Has this helped deepen your connection to the deity? After a month look at how you can improve your practice and make changes as needed.

CHAPTER FIVE

Unverified Personal Gnosis

When my dreams are just dreams, they fade easily upon waking. The details are fuzzy and unclear, they melt away with the morning sun. When my dreams are not dreams, when they are something else, they are as clear to me upon waking as a memory of something in the waking world. This dream is one of those.

I get out of my car because there are flowers falling all around it. Although I apparently drove here, "here" is a relative term since the landscape is made up of solely one thing: flowers. White flowers floating through the air lazily, their sweet smell like nothing I have smelled before. The perfume is pungent yet not overly sweet. It soothes me down to my depths. There are white flower petals on the ground as well. I can't tell if there is dirt or rock or grass below them. All I see are flowers, in the air or covering things, or floating in swirls around wherever it is that I am. But there is something else too. Blodeuwedd is here. The Welsh goddess created from flowers. At first, she has no form other than the flowers, then some of the flowers falling through the air take on the shape of a white owl. It is beautiful but it strikes me that in every dream where Blodeuwedd has appeared, it is never as a woman. She is always the flowers of her origin or in the shape of the owl, the shape she was given as a punishment. I think perhaps that is sad. She is never free. But I feel her laugh at my thought. "Free? How am I not free?" She asks in a voice that is everywhere at once. "The shape of the woman was my cage. I existed before they took my flowers to shape me into the image of their desire. The woman was the mask. I have always been the flowers, been of the earth, of the wild, untamed and raw places. I returned when I became the owl. From the earth and wild I came, and back to it I returned. But my sorrows gave me a new shape. I am no longer soft as new petals. I see into dark places now; I have sharp talons to rip and tear. But I am not caged or punished or afraid."

I am struck by her words and it jars me awake and out of the dream. In her stories Blodeuwedd is punished. She was made by a magician from wildflowers, to be a bride for a man who could not take a wife from humankind. She is transformed into an owl for trying to both leave and murder a husband she did not want. Her words give me a new understanding to a story I already know. I never considered she existed before the magician's spell. That her spirit was there in the wild and was plucked up and reshaped because someone else needed a loophole to give Lleu a wife. I had never considered that becoming the owl was her way to return to whence she came. It's not a perspective you'll find in the lore. It's all unverified person gnosis, something I believe because of what this goddess has told me. You don't have to agree with me on it. You don't have to believe that Blodeuwedd herself imparted it to me. Yet that dream, that gnosis, has shaped how I connect with her and how I view her story to this day.

Unverified Personal Gnosis or UPG goes hand in hand with working directly with deity. Gnosis comes from the Greek root meaning "knowing" or "knowledge." Personal, being that it is both a personal belief and that it is received during a personal experience, such as journey work, or meditation. Unverified of course means that it is information you cannot prove to be true. Maybe it really came from deity or maybe it was your ego or higher self talking. In short it is information that a deity or spirit has imparted to you that cannot be verified.

UPG can be anything from the messages the gods impart to us, to instructions we received from the gods on how to make offerings. This includes a wide range of information from something you are instructed to do by deity in your personal practices to messages directly imparted to you by deity through journey work. It can also be information we receive in dreams, ritual or visionary experiences. If you think about it, information received this way makes up a really big chunk of modern Pagan practice. What makes UPG complicated is how we choose to process the information we receive. The gods aren't always direct or clear in their messages. Some interpretation is required and at times, a grain of salt is needed. Some UPG can have significance to the wider community, and sometimes the knowledge we receive is deeply personal and relates only to our own spiritual development. As much as we don't want to admit it, other times UPG just might be our egos talking to us and not the gods at all. Sounds complicated, right?

In general, there are two types of UPG. The first type relates to the worship of a deity. It might fill in gaps in knowledge relating to a deity. Some cultures and pantheons have a great deal of information about taboos, proper steps to worship their gods and intact mythology that remains to them. In others all that may be left to us through time is a deity's name and nothing more. For many who worship deities where there is little lore or information left about them, UPG can be a vital tool to create a living practice to honor that deity. For others it can fill in gaps in knowledge that are not explained in the lore. For example, the Irish goddess Danu has no stories about her that remain to us. There are things named after her like the Danube river and the title for the Irish gods, The Tuatha De Danann, includes her name but there is literally zero mythology or lore left to tell us who she is or what she was associated with. Yet there are still many people who worship her. They use information they feel has been directly given to them from Danu to build a modern practice.

This kind of gnosis can also be information about a deity's likes or dislikes, such as what offerings they want to receive, a deity's personality, or what a deity looks like. In many cases this can be a shared gnosis with devotees who do not know each other all receiving the same or similar information. For example, a friend of mine who worships Hekate felt she was told that she needed to be veiled while making offerings at her altar to Hekate and that she needed to walk backwards to depart from the altar space so she was not turning her back to the goddess. There is no historical information regarding priests being veiled when worshiping Hekate. So, we cannot say this is a historical practice, only that Hekate herself wants this to be part of her worship. Interestingly, I have met two other priestesses of Hekate who did not know each other who both have been given almost the same instructions from Hekate. Similarly, most worshipers of the Morrigan believe whiskey is her preferred offering, even though there is nothing historical that supports that. Yet they feel the Morrigan has directed them to make it part of her worship. I'm sure you can probably think of more examples in your own practices. If you have ever felt directed by the gods to do or offer something, you have experienced this kind of UPG. Regardless whether it is a message or instruction, this kind of UPG has more to do with the deity than the individual. If the Morrigan wants to be worshiped a certain way she is going to tell many of her worshipers this information rather than just one individual.

The second type of gnosis relates to wisdom or insight into your own personal development, rather than being a greater universal statement about the gods. The "personal" part of UPG is important here. Usually this UPG has nothing to do with anyone except yourself. This can be a personal message where the wording had meaning to you, but to another person who worships the same deity it might have little or no meaning. Don't get me wrong, this type of gnosis can be invaluable. Most of the gnosis I experience on a regular basis falls into this category. Just because it only pertains to you doesn't mean it's not valuable. The lessons the gods teach us can't be all the same. Our lives aren't the same; we have different needs. We all have different strengths to develop, different weaknesses to overcome. The pitfalls of this type of gnosis usually is our own self-doubt and ego. Most people feel a strong desire to know what they are doing is correct. We equate correct with worthwhile. Therefore, even if a message is meaningful to us, we seek to validate that it is legitimate. That can happen in several ways. We might share the experiences with others and if they agree with our experiences, then they must be valid. When our ego gets in the way we might demand that others agree that what we experience has some bearing on their devotion to deity, in essence forcing our gnosis on others.

Many years ago, I was part of a group that circled together off and on during the year. One of the women in the group was close to the goddess Brigid. At one get-togethers she was telling others in the group about vivid dreams she was having where Brigid was appearing with owls. When she asked the then high priestess what connections there were between Brigid and owls, she was disappointed to be told there were none. When others in the group suggested the owl might be a symbol for something going on in her life, or perhaps represented herself, she became upset. She felt Brigid must be imparting some lost information to her, and that Brigid was now, and in some ancient lost past, an owl goddess. No other explanation was acceptable. Because any other explanation would invalidate the experience for her. It couldn't possibly be just a personal message; it had to be some grand important message Brigid wanted her to reveal to everyone. This unfortunately is not uncommon. The internet is full of examples of people who use their UPG as a basis to rewrite the correspondences or mythology of the gods. I'm sure the imagery this woman was experiencing was a message that would only have meaning to her, and that personal message was valid. I don't think she imagined the experience, or that Brigid wasn't talking to her. But the meaning of the message I think was lost. The thing is, we have to learn to be comfortable with the idea that some information we receive isn't going to pertain to the wider community. If you choose to share it with others that's fine, but they probably won't find the same meaning in it that you did. That doesn't make the experience any less valid, it's just personal. Most people are afraid to be wrong and when their opinion is challenged, they tend to dig their heels in and insist that their vision has some bearing on everyone else too. Because they feel it has to if it is indeed a valid vision or experience. And that is when UPG wars begin.

UPG Wars

All too often we fall into the trap of assuming all gnosis must be shared gnosis. That all the messages the gods impart upon us are meant for everyone. Shared UPG does exist. We find this in how followers of the same god who do not know each other or live thousands of miles apart pick up the same information from a deity. But most of the time, these aren't dire messages and relate to how a deity wants to be worshiped in today's world. That isn't to say that the gods don't bestow profound messages to us. I've experienced that often enough myself. But we must accept that if we share that profound message it may strike a chord with some or could even be completely repugnant to others who worship the same deity. Then the finger pointing starts. It becomes "My UPG is right and yours is wrong!" and accusations that the message one received is made up or totally bullshit begins.

The thing is, a message can be legitimately from the gods, and still just be for your ears. That's a hard thing for people to accept. We want validation, especially after an intense experience. We want to be the chosen one whom the gods speak their secrets to. Then on the flip side there are those of us who keep our experiences to ourselves and rarely share, fearing others will pick apart our experience and call it false. I do write about some of my experiences. But there are far more that I don't write about, not because I don't believe they were real but because they were intensely personal.

They belong only to me. I think in many ways sharing occult experiences can turn into a competition. If you didn't have a really cool vivid encounter with a deity or spirit, then somehow you are less of a priest or practitioner. You shouldn't feel obligated to share, or that you have to have a fantastic story to tell. Some things you might only reveal to a few close friends, or no one else at all. And that is a perfectly valid choice.

Perhaps the best example of a UPG war was one that played out for the most part online and almost succeeded in dividing a community. A well-known Druid group had a priest who had a very vivid visionary experience at a yearly gathering she was attending. She saw a vision of what she felt was the spirit of her religion, which manifested as a chained woman. In her vision she freed the spirit, ripping off the chains. She had some opinions on what that meant and that this spirit she saw in her vision should be worshiped as the embodiment of her Druid tradition. Afterwards she wrote about the experience and basically demanded that others in the group acknowledge her vision to be true. I am not a part of this Druid organization but have many friends who are, and as it was a very public dispute I just watched from the sidelines. What ensued was a full-fledged online UPG battle. Was the vision real? Did she make it up? If it's real, do we have to do something about this chained spirit of our tradition? Everyone had an opinion, and many people were upset about the opinions of others. This is certainly not the only or the last case of someone believing their UPG has to be shoved down the throats of others to matter. I personally think she really did have a valid visionary experience. But I think whatever the message was, it was meant for her and her own spiritual journey, rather than the entire organization. Sometimes something can be real, but just not be for everyone else.

The sad thing is that when this happens it often makes people second-guess their connection to their gods. It becomes a battle of who has the most interesting or outrageous UPG, and if you question someone else's experience then you must not be a "true" worshiper of that god. When it is a well-known Pagan or public figure making such claims, this becomes even more amplified. Because if so-and-so says it's true it must be true, right? They have the direct telephone line to the gods; how can they be wrong? When it comes to the intangible many of us have a strong need to be right. Because if we are wrong, what else do we believe in that's also wrong? The same goes for believing the UPG and experiences of our leaders and teachers.

Verifying UPG

So how do we verify something that by its very definition is unverifiable? There are a few ways we can get a better read on whether our UPG is legitimate or just wishful thinking. The first thing is look to the lore. Does anything in the lore surrounding that deity or the folklore of that culture support what you experienced? This has happened often in my own experiences, where I will see an image only to find something in folklore that supports it months later.

Divination is your next best go-to. If you don't trust yourself to read without bias, then ask someone you trust to read for you. Ask others who have a connection to that deity what they think. If you go this route you have to keep in mind, they may not agree with your UPG. Keep an open mind and in some cases, you might find that others have received the same information. Don't be disappointed if they haven't. Listen to their thoughts and perspectives and see if there is anything there that you didn't think of. Also don't jump to conclusions. Ask yourself: Is this what I want to hear? Because if the gods are telling you exactly what you want to hear, chances are it's too good to be true. Again, divination will bring some clarity if this is the case. You can also ask the gods to send you additional signs to confirm the information you are perceiving is true.

Testing out the information is also a way to find validation. If you have been told to make a certain type of offering, do a ritual a particular way or during a certain time, try it out. Did it work well? If yes, then you are probably on the right track. If you read any of Morgan Daimler's works, she tells a story about receiving a recipe in a dream for a small offering cake the sidhe wanted her to make. Not being someone who normally just creates a recipe, she tried it out to see if what she was told would even produce something edible. It did and she continued to use it because it worked.

Taking a healthy look at our own egos is required when we experience a UPG. There is nothing wrong with a little skepticism. In the end only you can keep your ego in check. Look at the information from all angles. Eliminate different possibilities. Take a healthy look at your motives in relation to a message that is received. A good rule of thumb is the phrase "extraordinary claims require extraordinary proof." What qualifies as extraordinary proof is up to you. If you receive a message, then the gods keep sending you similar messages and exasperatingly keep pointing you in a certain direction, that might qualify as your extraordinary evidence. It all depends on you.

Writing down your experiences is also a helpful way to verify at a later date. Wording can be easily forgotten after a while, as can other details. Visionary experiences can have a dream-like quality and details can fade quickly. Keep an open mind and don't always expect to get validation right away. In one case, it took me years to verify something I had seen in journey work. A friend was facilitating a ritual where we did a guided meditation and went to a certain area along the world tree and encountered Odin. At one point we were told to leave an offering to Odin beside his throne. As I did so Odin quickly snatched up my hand and drew a rune on it. It was a little startling and certainly not in the "script" of the meditation my friend was facilitating during the ritual. Afterwards I drew the symbol on paper so I would remember it. At that time, I knew nothing about runes and asked my friend if it was an actual rune or something else. She said it looked similar to Odin's rune, Ansuz, but it was slightly different, with an extra line on the top. She surmised it was my own "personal" rune that Odin had given me. I didn't really know what to think about it for a long time. I didn't really think my own personal rune felt like the right answer, but she gave me some information about the meaning of Ansuz and that was a start at least. Then several years later another friend whose focus is the Norse gods looked at the drawing after we had talked about the experience and instantly recognized it to be one of the Anglo-Saxon runes, which do look slightly different than the Elder Futhark that most people are familiar with. I had never doubted the experience, it had felt valid to me, it just took me a while to understand the message. That it was an Anglo-Saxon rune was a kind of validation. I saw something that I didn't even know existed, it hadn't been something I imagined. I suspect discovering what it was came at a time when I was ready to understand the message better. Gnosis doesn't bring instant understanding. Be open to the idea that just because a message is given, it doesn't mean understanding will be immediate.

Ultimately when it comes to UPG we have to keep an open mind. Some of the information the gods gift us with can be verified, and some of it we must take on faith. Things that may seem profound and earthshattering to you may be exactly that, but just for you. Check your ego and don't try to force your UPG on others. UPG can be invaluable and can guide our spiritual practices, but like anything we need to be able to take a step back and take a hard look at what we experience and decide how to process and use that information.

Suggested Exercises

1. Examine some of your own examples of personal gnosis. How have they influenced your beliefs and practices?
2. Come up with a plan to verify gnosis for yourself. What resources can you use to verify lore? What divination system would be your go-to for verification?

A Ritual of Devotion

You Will Need

An offering

A candle

Prayer you have created

Image of deity

The purpose of this ritual is to welcome the presence of deity into your life and your intent to honor them in your spiritual practice. It is a kind of energetic welcome, where you are reaching out to deity. It can be used as a beginning step in building a devotional practice with the deity you choose. Perhaps it is a deity that you wish to know better, or maybe the presence of a deity has started showing up in your life and you wish to recognize that presence and build a connection.

This ritual is just an example for you to build upon. Any ritual to a specific deity should in some way be tailored to that deity. You will likely be adding to it to fit your devotional style and the deity in question. Feel free to change it to fit your needs. It does require that you have done some of the exercises and techniques in part one.

You will need an image, statue, or representation of the deity you will be honoring. It doesn't have to be big or elaborate but just something that symbolizes that deity to you personally. If you don't not have an image or symbol to represent deity, you can also use the candle. Select a candle color or scent related to deity. You will also need to identify an appropriate offering for the deity you will be honoring. In addition to that you will need to create a prayer for the deity. You will also need a bowl or dish of some kind to place your offering in. Additionally, it would be beneficial to arrange items, using colors or scents that you know are associated with or appealing to the deity in your ritual space. You will also need your preferred divination system on hand, cards, etc.

You could do this ritual in front of an altar you have created for the deity, or you can do this in a more formal ritual setting. Use whatever opening and closing for the ritual that you prefer.

Take a few minutes to clearly see the deity in your mind. What do they look like? Are there images, symbols, scents that represent their presence to you? Send out your intention to welcome and honor the deity, your desire to have them as a part of your life. When you are ready light the candle and raise your hands, palm up, saying:

> *I honor you,* (name of deity)
> *I seek to know you more fully*
> *I seek your presence within my life*
> *I welcome you*
> *I make this offering of* (whatever you are offering)
> *to you this day*

Hold up the item you are offering. If it is a libation pour it into the offering bowl, or if it is food or some other item place it reverently in the dish or bowl you have set aside for it.

At this point you should recite the prayer you created to honor the deity. Spend some more time connecting to deity and letting yourself be open to any messages from the divine. Use your preferred divination system to confirm your offering was accepted, and for any additional messages from deity.

Close the ritual in whatever way you choose.

PART TWO

Dedicant

Our relationships with the gods can be quite diverse. There are those who see this relationship as something akin to parent/child, others as deity/servant, mentor/mentee, or even deity/spouse, and countless more. The personalities of the deity and our own also play a part in how these interactions evolve. How we interact with one deity may differ greatly from how we connect with another. We have looked at the mechanics of building a devotional practice; now we will go one step deeper and look at what it means to be dedicated to a deity.

Once we know how to build the connections and interact with these beings, the real complexities of this work come into play. There is nothing that says that you have to delve deeper into the woods of devotional work. You may be happy and fulfilled just building a relationship with a deity as a devotee. It doesn't make you any better or worse as a Pagan. It's a personal choice and anyone who demands you must find or pick a deity to dedicate to isn't doing you any favors. Dedication changes the relationship and can have a far deeper impact on your everyday day life than you might realize.

Dedicating or making a formal commitment, oath, or agreements with a deity is not an uncommon practice in Paganism. Yet I think we fail in informing those who take on this process with what it truly entails, or the risks involved. For many of us we might have read about the process in a book or saw a dedication ritual online or found one from our favorite author and thought, I've got to get all the Pagan merit badges! Everyone else has one, this is the next step in my spiritual practice! And then we say oaths, make promises to the gods and our entire world gets shaken up and turned inside out, and we are in deep unknown waters unsure how to get back to shore.

In my own experience people tend to jump into making bargains or proclaiming oaths to spiritual beings with the cavalier attitude of a new year's resolution. A grand proclamation when we are heady with the energy of ritual may sound great, but there are consequences to our words. What distinguishes a devotee from a dedicant is quite simple. While a devotee has a practice of honoring and communicating with a spirit or god, a dedicant has given some kind of oath, or entered into a binding agreement for a period of time with a spirit or power. The thing is, oaths matter. No matter how seriously or lightly you say an oath to a deity, those words are like an invisible tattoo. You might forget they are there, to you it might have been in the heat of the moment, but the power you have offered them to does not. If ignored or not left fulfilled there will be real-world consequences.

There are a variety of oaths and agreements one can enter into with a spiritual being. It is not limited to the gods per say, as I know several people who have very profound dedications to ancestral beings, angelic beings, and the sidhe. Their oaths to these beings

have had just as much of a dramatic effect on their lives and practices as those I know whose agreements are with beings we consider gods. In many ways gods seem to be more lenient, as anyone
who has ever bargained with the fair folk can attest to. If we look
at the stories passed down to us in folklore, breaking promises
to the sidhe usually involved falling asleep for a hundred years or
meeting a terrible death.

On the other side of things, having a dedication to a deity
comes with the benefit of deeper connection and understanding of
that being. It is a new level of intimacy. It could be compared to
casual dating vs. moving in together. Just as there is that friend you
love but you both would murder each other if you lived in the same
apartment, when it comes to gods it's important to think carefully
about who you enter into such agreements with.

CHAPTER SIX

When the Gods Call

I think I might have a goddess stalking me. Ok maybe stalking is the wrong word. But I'm being stalked by her animal minions at very least. I have encountered the Morrigan in a dream, not knowing if the name she gave me was the name of an actual goddess. At this time, I'm fairly new to the ins and outs of working with gods. The few mentions of her I find in books warn against connecting with her. Yet I feel drawn to her. I've called on her in ritual and the experience has been very moving and meaningful. Yet I am pretty green as a Pagan, shouldn't I listen to those who know better than I do? I'm not really sure what to make of it all. So, after my first few rituals I've kind of stopped trying to connect with this supposedly dangerous goddess. Maybe what I was sensing wasn't what I thought it was? Except the Morrigan isn't done making her presence known.

I grab a bagel before running out the door to go to work. I'm running late, but I stop in my tracks as the slamming of the front door sends what looks like a flock of crows scattering into the air. They were perched on my car, on the garbage can in the driveway, on the roof and in the trees around the house. It's the third time this week I have encountered something similar outside. I get in the car and tell myself maybe someone has been leaving the garbage can lid slightly open when the trash was put out? It isn't weird that crows hang out near easy-to-pick-at garbage; they are scavengers after all. That is a logical and sound explanation.

I get in to work and clock in. It is summer and while it hasn't been particularly hot the last few days, today is a pretty solid ninety something. My co-workers inform me the air conditioning is still not working. We didn't mind it so much last month, but it's definitely time they got someone out to figure out what is wrong with it. So we all don't suffocate in the office, we prop the front door open and open all the windows. Luckily the office is in a strip mall and on the first level so it's easy to keep the door open and get a nice breeze.

I start on a report and it isn't long before the unsettling number of crows outside my house is forgotten. Then I hear a "Caw!" It's oddly close. I look up and my jaw drops. In front of my desk is a crow. Not in my mind's eye or some kind of waking vision. It's literally right there. Looking at me. It calls out again. "Caw, caw! Caw, caw!" Later my co-worker will tell me it just waltzed in from the parking lot and through the open front door. I just keep staring at the crow, frozen and open mouthed. My boss interprets this as I'm afraid of the bird and attempts to shoo the bird out the door again. By this point the rest of my co-workers are laughing or commenting on the commotion. The crow decides it has accepted my boss's challenge and proceeds to fly anywhere except out the door. It takes a good twenty minutes for him to herd the crow back *outside again. Somewhere in the back of my mind I think I can perceive a woman laughing.*

I know enough to know that I don't have to give in when a god calls to someone. There is a choice. Ignoring things in this case apparently does not count as a choice. At least not to this goddess. I think about what I have sensed about her vs. the advice I've read in regard to her. I kind of feel like the Fool in the tarot, about to walk off a cliff not knowing if I will fly or fall. I thought I was the one who chose which god I wanted to have a relationship with. But that feels too much like ordering something off a fast-food menu. I'm starting to realize that sometimes the gods call to you, not the other way around. Sometimes they just show up in our lives and when we think we can ignore them they send crows to remind you they are still there waiting. Waiting for you to choose if you are going to listen to their call.

Dedicating to a deity is not about deciding you really, really like a god or goddess and therefore you must adopt them as your patron deity. Usually you don't do the choosing at all.

In Neo-Paganism many who have a dedication to deity will tell you that the deity in question chose them. The deity may have been in the shadows and in the periphery of their perception for a long time, until they acknowledge their presence. So, what do we do when the gods call to us? How do we know when we feel the call of a deity? Do we have a choice? How do we navigate these agreements with the gods?

If you haven't had much experience working with deity, it can be rather thrilling when they show up, especially when it's in a dramatic way. There is a sense of awe when something so much bigger than ourselves appears as an active participant in our lives. We assume that if Thor shows up in our lives, we are obligated to give him what he wants. But it's important to keep in mind you always have a choice. If the gods could order us around, we would all be robots. We have free will, and that is a part of our soul, our essence, that even the gods can't touch. Only you have control over that piece of you. And yes, even you, puny mortal, can say no to a god. It would go better for you if you say no politely, but the point remains, you have a choice.

So, you might be thinking, what's the big deal? What does it matter how many or which gods I dedicate to? What's the worst that can happen? Well, a lot can happen. When you have dedicative relationships with deity, you become the representative of that deity in the world. They can take a more heavy-handed approach in making you a better person, a person more like them, a person who fits their agendas in the world. Many Heathen trads will not do public ritual because they do not believe in mixing their wyrd with people they do not know well or are not vetted. They see their wyrd as a person's energy, the threads of their fate, which can mix with others for good or ill. Having a dedication to a deity is much like that. You are mixing the spider web of your energy, your fate, your wyrd, with that being. That changes you, and that change can be for good or ill. At least it can be for ill from our perspective. The gods give us exactly what we ask for at times, and sometimes we don't realize that what we are asking them for might not be what we really need or want. Asking for positive change in one's life sounds good enough, but when it requires you to make very real and difficult changes in your life, it doesn't seem as good of an idea anymore.

Having a dedication to a deity is not something to be jumped into lightly. In general, these are permanent relationships. Ones in which you both experience a deeper relationship to deity and become a representative of that deity in the wider world. There are rewards here, just as there is danger. The first thing you must accept if you embark on such a relationship with deity is that it will change you, and in many ways that is the whole point anyway. Becoming closer to a deity requires we understand the lessons they embody and learn to connect to the forces they hold sway over. It is a kind of alchemy.

A common misconception when one makes oaths to a deity is that this instantly makes you a priest of said god/dess. While it certainly puts us on a path towards priesthood, having a dedication to a deity doesn't make you a priest. Dedication is a private relationship with deity. You may share your experiences with others who are devoted to that god or goddess, but you are not facilitating the experiences of others through ritual or other mediums. Like a devotee who worships a god, the experience is still something that has its focus on yourself and your journey with the gods.

Do the Gods Choose? Or Do I Choose?

Many times, people will become attracted to a deity that is connected to something they like and assume that said deity should be their patron. But the deity who calls to you most likely won't be the one you are expecting or one you would have chosen yourself. After all, not only must we be willing to offer our dedication to deity, but that deity in turn must be willing to accept our oaths and dedication as well. Just because you admire the qualities of a deity doesn't automatically mean they should be your patron.

I've been horse obsessed since I was a child, and in my early days of being a Pagan I had myself convinced that Epona was going to be the deity that would be a big part of my life. I wrote one of my first rituals in honor of her. Picked an auspicious day, spoke my beautifully written invocation, and poured my offerings. Imagine my surprise when I felt nothing. Well, almost nothing. There was just the barest of begrudged acknowledgement. As if she was saying, "Um, this is nice and all, but I've got nothing to say to you." Just because I was certain I should have a connection to her, didn't make her receptive. In the end, she wasn't what I needed, even though I couldn't see it at the time.

How Do I Know if a Deity is Trying to Get My Attention?

There isn't a guaranteed formula to this one. It's something you have to feel out for yourself. Usually when a deity is courting you, you will encounter symbols and animals connected to them. If you keep encountering the same things and it's too often to be a coincidence, it's time to start paying attention. You could come across their name several times on TV, in a book etc. It's ok to be skeptical as well. Ask yourself the hard questions. Is this really what I want to hear? Is it just a coincidence? Are there other explanations?

The next step is to start doing some research. Learn about the deity in question, their symbols and their culture. Know who you are dealing with before you go any further.

Divination is also essential, especially if you are second-guessing yourself. Use whatever divination tool you prefer and ask if XYZ deity is really present. Why are they showing up now? What will this kind of devotional relationship mean for you in the future? If you don't trust yourself, ask a friend or reader you trust to do the divination for you.

Speaking to other followers of that god is also a good idea. Someone who already has a deep relationship with that deity can give you a better idea of what to expect. Learning from their experiences can help you avoid pitfalls and give you a clearer idea of how involved with the deity you wish to be. Having some idea of what you are getting yourself into will help you determine if this is right for you.

Doing some of the work we discussed in the first part of this book with that deity will also help. Just because a deity shows up doesn't mean you shouldn't get to know them a bit before you decide to make them your patron deity.

Saying No

Believe it or not you really do have that option. Saying no might mean that deity's presence in your life diminishes or goes away completely. But better that than making promises you don't feel are right for you or ones you don't think you can keep. Don't be afraid to negotiate.

A lot of people assume that if a god swoops in and shows up in their lives that they must automatically dedicate to them as a patron deity. Or if you have a particularly intense experience with a god that you must accept and do what they are telling you to do. I think we can still be in awe of the gods, and at the same time recognize that they have their own agendas. Just because a deity wants you to do something doesn't mean you don't have a choice in the matter.

Having a dedication might be something that you want to explore later down the road, but just isn't on the table at the moment. Remember you have free will, and even the gods can't take that away from you. Saying no may also be negotiating your own terms. You might only be offering your time and devotion for a certain length of time or have set limits. Or there might be specific conditions you set with deity before taking the relationship further.

How You View the Relationship Matters

A lot of people see both dedication and priesthood almost as a kind of enslavement. Being in service to a deity isn't the same as being a servant. In general, I find that if you view yourself as the property of a deity, then they tend to treat you as such. This depends a bit on the deity, but it's not a good mindset to have regardless. Take time to consider what having a dedication to a deity means to you. What does that relationship look like to you? Are you opening yourself up to a deity having more influence in your life? Absolutely. But you should have a clear understanding of why you want that or what you want from that deepened intimacy.

Will I Have to Give Up the Other Gods I Feel Close To?

This is a common question. Many people feel that they have to cut ties or stop worshiping the other gods they have felt close to when they take on a patron deity. Having a dedication to a deity makes you no less a polytheist. Paganism implies that one may worship many gods, so you should not feel like you must stop worshiping the other deities that are part of your practice when another god shows up. What is important to keep in mind is that you don't stop making offerings to the other gods you have a connection with. If you give them their due, and keep up whatever your normal offerings or practice is with them in addition to your worship of a new deity you feel called to, you are not likely to run into problems. Issues usually arise when you put all your focus into connecting with one deity and the one you used to connect to has an altar collecting dust. We all probably have that friend who tends to vanish when they get into a new romantic relationship. They get consumed in the new relationship and ignore the other people in their life. It's not unlike that. Like any relationship we have to cultivate and feed all of our relationships, divine or otherwise. That requires time management and putting the effort into making time for everyone. For those in unconventional or non-monogamous relationships, you might already be familiar with this concept.

For myself there are certain days and times I make offerings to different deities that I have a dedication to. It might be a certain day of the week or a certain moon cycle; all that is important is that you are consistent. The only issue I have ever run into is that for whatever reason one deity may not want their altar space in the same area of the room as another god's altar. You can usually pick up pretty quickly if the energy between the two are not happy. Then you can negotiate a new place for one of the two altars.

Can I Get Out of It?

Again, dedicating and making oaths to the gods is not something we should take lightly. In general, that is so because most of the time the bargain is permanent. If you are going to dedicate to a god, you need to be willing to give some part of yourself and life over to that deity. You are mixing that web of fate, your wyrd, with that being. It is not unheard of for a deity to release someone from a dedication or oath. It certainly happens, but there is almost always a cost. A price to be paid or offered to mark that ending. What is important to remember is that it most likely won't be your decision to end the dedication. Your oaths are to the gods and it's their choice in the end, both to accept it in the first place and to break it if they see fit. It's like getting a tattoo. It's permanent. Maybe it fades or you get a cover-up. Maybe a laser can remove it, but either way that marking is going to be part of your skin forever. And if it's not, it won't be too easy to erase it.

Being Dedicated to a God Makes Me Special

Having a dedication to a deity doesn't make us better than anyone else. It also doesn't mean we have a perfect understanding of that deity. Just because Odin accepted your oath doesn't mean you are now his mouthpiece in the world. Many times, others look to a person who has a dedicative relationship with a deity for a direct phone line to that deity. They assume because that person has a deep relationship with that god that they have all the answers and can speak for that deity. This kind of thinking is dangerous and often is abused. Remember, just because someone says they are dedicated to a deity doesn't mean they really are. Dedication in no way means the gods have shared the secrets of the universe with you. Ego comes into play here, and we just have to learn to identify and avoid the people who think their dedications make them more important than others. The gods don't have messiahs in my opinion. They talk to whomever they wish, and they take into their service whomever they wish. Sometimes they just take someone who is useful to them. Useful doesn't necessarily make someone a good person; it just means they can fulfill something that deity is interested in. If you don't have many applicants for the job, sometimes you just take what's available.

Suggested Exercises

1. Consider how you realized the presence of deity in your life. When was it? What clues or signs made you aware of the presence of the divine?

2. Have your experiences with a deity you chose to dedicate to differed from the experiences with those who showed up without you seeking them?

3. How has having a dedication to deity impacted your practices?

CHAPTER SEVEN

Oaths, Vows & Prohibitions

The priestesses gather in the temple. It is not always a temple, but when we gather yearly at this place, we transform the small building into one. One of our group has contacted us, asking us to help facilitate a formal dedication to the Morrigan and to witness her oath to the Great Queen. The priestesses have been swapping email messages and planning something we think will be meaningful and special.

One of the priestesses speaks with the dedicant outside in a field. They do a brief meditation, preparing for what is to come. Then she guides her to the temple. The other priestesses wait there to greet her. They hold items, symbols that hold importance to the one offering her oath. She holds the items the priestesses offer, and they speak words of blessing and advice. They challenge her, and she acknowledges these challenges and faces each.

The dedicant makes offerings at the altars. Whiskey is poured, incense burned. I feel the presence of the Morrigan, she is here too, to witness and if she chooses to accept the oath. The dedicant has spoken to all of the priestesses, held all the symbols. She is given a final poetic blessing, then it is time for her to say her oath. It is thought out. Words we have asked her to spend a great deal of time crafting and considering. She says them from memory, offering them to the Morrigan as we stand witness. More offerings are made, and I feel that the Morrigan is pleased. The oath is accepted. The priestesses acknowledge this, bearing witness. It is more than just facilitating or observing. On some level we are part of that oath too. This is a member of our community and by bearing witness to her words we have an obligation to help her fulfill her promise. To help her along her path to the goddess we all serve. Oaths are powerful. The gods expect us to make good on our words, to hold true to them. Witnessing an oath has a power to it as well. You are witness to a usually unbreakable promise, and in many ways witnessing an oath can be as binding as being the one who speaks it. You hold not only the knowledge of the words offered to the gods but the obligation to help the speaker fulfill their word as best as you can.

Since the defining aspect of a devotee is that they have offered oaths or vows to the divine, it is only fair to take a look at the definitions of these terms. An oath is a promise, usually made before witnesses or some kind of authority, as a guarantee that an action will be done. It could be to tell the truth or that you will serve a community in a certain capacity, such as when a public official takes an oath of service. A vow is a promise to take certain actions or uphold certain values.

Many use oath and vow interchangeably, and in some cases they can be. Both are promises, and both, when broken, can have consequences. But there is a subtle difference. Generally, a vow tends to be of a more personal nature and is usually offered to an individual rather than a larger group. One could offer either or both to a deity, depending on the circumstance. A promise to serve deity or do a task for deity could be something you do in private simply between yourself and deity, or it could be sworn in the presence of a group you work with or before a community. Whether you choose to call it an oath or vow is a personal choice, as the lines between are often blurred. For our purposes here, I use these terms interchangeably, as we are covering a wide variety of applications.

There are a variety of oaths and vows one may feel called to enter into with gods and spirits. Oaths, vows, and even spiritual prohibitions are all at their core promises. Promises and agreements we make with the divine for various reasons. There are oaths of service and priesthood that might span a lifetime. There are agreements one might enter into for a short amount of time, perhaps for a specific task. Sometimes these promises are solely between ourselves and deity, while in other cases those who witness our promises have obligations to help us see our task through to the end. In short, oaths and vows can be complicated.

I tend to think of oaths as a kind of contract. Like any contract there are obligations on both parties involved; there may be specific stipulations and time frames involved. There may be loopholes and clauses about not fulfilling the contract, etc. If we frame it this way in our minds I think we are less likely to see oaths as meaningless things we can break. They aren't something we promise to do on a whim. They are covenants between the gods and ourselves. The gods expect us to keep our end of the bargain. No matter what culture you look at, stories involving breaking one's word to a deity never result in a happy ending. The person in question either has a horrible misfortune afterwards or in many cases forfeits their life.

In many cultures how an oath was taken was a ritualized process, and in many cases involved the oath being taken upon an object. This is not unlike our modern concept of swearing an oath of office or an oath to tell the truth in court on a Bible. The oath is made more valid by it being done when invoking a god to witness it and when said while touching or in the presence of a sacred object. Swords and other weapons historically have been popular items to swear oaths upon, asking that the weapon break or turn against its wielder if they break their word. We can see this in *The Cattle Raid of Cooley*, an Irish saga, where the warrior Fergus swears an oath upon his sword, naming it as a sacred object of the goddess Macha. Similarly, the *Landnámabók* recounts that an oath ring was kept at temples of the Norse gods. Although called a ring it was much larger than something worn on the finger, instead being something the priest wore as a bracelet or arm ring. It was held when swearing oaths and invoking the gods to witness the oath and had the blood of sacrificial animals put on it. "A ring, weighting two ounces or more, was to lie on the altar in every chief temple. Every priest had to wear that ring on his arm at all legal assemblies that he himself should discharge and redden it beforehand in the gore [blood] of the animal that he himself sacrificed there. Any man who has legal business to discharge at court first had to swear an oath on that ring and call two or more witnesses."[1] It is also relayed in the *Landnámabók* that certain gods would be called on to witness the oath as well, particularly Freyr and Njord.

In general, there are three types of oaths modern Pagans might encounter in their practices: oaths of reciprocity, oaths of service, and spiritual prohibitions. Although, as we will discuss later, this isn't always considered an oath depending on the tradition one works within.

Oaths of Reciprocity

Oaths of reciprocity can also be considered bargains or short-term agreements with deity. They are made with the understanding that you give, so deity may give. This might be a promise to do a specific task for a deity or give a specific offering so that the deity may grant you a boon. The idea behind this is that the boon you are asking for is much easier for the higher power you are contacting to be able to bring about. Thus, both parties are giving something of value to the other, and something that is within their abilities to give. Being specific about what you are offering to give or do for a deity is crucial, in this or any oath. Specific time frames would be helpful, as well as statements that include "within my ability to do/give." Also, when offering an oath you have to go into it understanding there will be consequences to breaking your word. If you give an oath that you aren't really capable of fulfilling, the deity really isn't going to care that you bit off more than you can chew. For example if you made a vow to Thor that you are going to make him an offering every day for a week so that he can help

---

1. Jakob Benediktsson, trans. *Íslendingabók, Landnámabók* (Hið Íslenzka Fornri-tafélag, 1968), 313–315.

you with a personal battle, but you only give him offerings three days out of seven, then you are breaking your oath. Maybe you can make additional offerings to appease this misstep, but it isn't likely he is going to offer his aid, and you have shown that keeping your word has little value to you. Make bargains and vows you can keep, and make them with the intention of keeping them.

Oaths of Service

Oaths or vows of service are probably the ones we are the most familiar with. These are the kinds of vows one would make when formally dedicating to a deity as a patron. It can also be a vow of priesthood or offering to serve a deity in a particular capacity. They usually do not specify a time frame, although they can be for a set amount of time. The majority of the time they are usually understood to be lifelong, unless the deity indicates otherwise. These kinds of oaths often mark a deepening of one's connection with a deity. You may be asked to do a specific task for that deity or make them your primary focus in your spiritual practice.

Every oath of service will be different, as every deity may ask different things of each of us. As a priestess of the Morrigan one aspect of my oath to the Great Queen is to help others connect and understand her. When I made that oath I didn't realize where fulfilling it would lead me. I had been a priestess for a while, when I got the specific instruction from the Morrigan to write a book about her. I did, and then as a result of that I started teaching more publicly. The more I taught, the more I kept getting a nudge that she wanted me to create an event that focused on her, a place where her devotees could gather, connect, and learn. Then I created a yearly retreat for the Morrigan. All those things were born from that oath of service. The Morrigan guided and nudged me towards the things she wanted me to do. Sometimes a clear specific direction was given, other times it was very fluid, and I was just in the right place at the right time to do something for her. A friend of mine who is dedicated to Airmid and Dian Cecht opened her own holistic healing practice as a part of her oaths of service as a priestess of these Irish gods of healing. In both these cases our offer of service to the gods is open ended and doesn't end with a single task; it is an ongoing thing. In some cases a deity may tell you specifically what they want you to do in their name, and other times it is something you are guided towards along your journey with that deity. Oaths of service don't have to be big grand gestures; sometimes they are simple things. I know another priestess whose service to Brigid is tending her flame for a certain number of nights a week. At first glance this can be seen as a type of devotional activity, which it is, but to her holding space for Brigid and honoring her in this way is part of her service to the goddess. It is not something that needs to be seen by others. It is more about bringing the goddess's energy into the world and partaking in something that has been done in the distant past to honor Brigid and continuing that tradition.

The difficulties many have navigating such oaths of service are making them work with their other devotions. Many people fear that having multiple dedications to many deities might anger some of the gods they already have a dedication or devotional relationship with. Other times folks might worry that taking a patron deity and making an oath to that deity, will upset other deities one calls upon but doesn't have a specific oath to. Many people feel they needed to ritually sever all bonds to one deity in order to have a dedication to another deity they felt was calling to them.

So, can one be dedicated to and have oaths of service to multiple deities? Absolutely. The oaths one makes to each deity will likely be quite different in nature. Pagans by their very nature will worship many gods, and it is not that uncommon to have oaths of service or priesthood made to more than one god or goddess. The important thing is to uphold your agreements with all of them. Don't stop making your offerings to one deity just because another god has suddenly shown up in your life. If you suddenly ignored the deity you made regular offerings and devotions to in favor of another deity, then yes, you'll more than likely have problems. As long as everyone is given their due there is no reason that having multiple oaths and dedications to deities can't work.

Spiritual Prohibitions

Most religions feature some kind of spiritual prohibition as part of their religious devotion. In many cases adhering to these prohibitions has less to do with making the promise directly to a deity, but more to do with taking them on as part of becoming a follower of a deity and that deity's religion. For example, Christians as part of their devotion to their deity will give up certain food items during Lent. Practitioners of Orthodox Judaism eat Kosher food and refrain from having sex with a woman while she is menstruating and seven days after. Adherence to these prohibitions are both part of being a member of that faith and done to show devotion to one's chosen deity. This can be true of anyone who is dedicated to a deity, regardless of the religion in question. As part of your dedication you may be instructed to avoid certain foods or activities as an act of devotion or respect for that deity. That direction might come from deity itself or from the religious community or group you are a part of.

A friend shared a story of a mishap with one such prohibition that was taken on by a group for a year. The prohibition was to not engage in sexual relations during a particular moon phase. Of course, a young man in the group went to a festival that year which just happened to be during that moon phase and ignoring the prohibition, spent the night with a woman he met at the event. No one will know, right? As it turns out he ended up contracting an STD from the woman. He went to the doctor and remedied the situation, but it was seen as the result of breaking his word to the gods.

In the Irish tradition there is a similar concept called a geis (plural geas) which is a taboo or spiritual prohibition that is placed on heroes and kings by a deity or Otherworldly being. In the case of a geis the person who breaks it usually forfeits their life, and there are many stories in Irish mythology that focus on the disastrous outcomes from breaking one's geis.

Spiritual prohibitions are a grey area. I tend to view them as something somewhat separate from an oath. Yet they are still related. An oath is something you promise to do, while a prohibition is something you are promising *not* to do. Despite the difference, it is still important to understand how each works. If you made an oath to a deity that you would abstain from a certain behavior, not eat a certain type of food, etc. and you freely offered this as an act of respect and reverence, then it could be seen either as an oath, since it is freely offered, or as a prohibition, since something is being abstained from.

While in the above story the group chose to take on a different prohibition yearly to show their devotion to their gods, in many of these cases, such as a geis, you might not be the one doing the choosing. When a prohibition is placed upon you, like a geis, that deity is specifically telling you the behavior you can't do. It's not initially your idea, thus many would not strictly consider this an oath. From my personal perspective prohibitions placed on you are a completely different animal since you didn't initiate the process. Not all spiritual prohibitions fall into this category; most are things people or religions take on willingly to show their dedication to the divine or their faith. But it is important to understand that some, like a geis, are not something sought by the individual and often don't work by the same rules, or even fit into the same category. With an oath at least you are writing the details of the contract, rather than having a contract handed to you with you having little to do with the wording, expectations, and rules of that promise.

When Oaths are Broken

While this should be avoided, at times unforeseen circumstances, health issues, and other factors might result in you unintentionally breaking your word. In general, unintentional slips seem to be dealt with less harshly than ones done intentionally. For example, I have to make a specific kind of offering to Badb, a few drops of blood, before doing any rituals involving her. Usually this is done in private at my home altar, even if the ritual is happening elsewhere, for safety and health reasons. There have been a few times when doing rituals where I was traveling or camping and forgot to do this. The business of getting dressed and ready for ritual just made me completely forget. In these cases, I have found that I had cut myself accidently on something in the woods or during the ritual, such as a rock or a briar bush, only to look down and see that I was bleeding. That was when it hit me that I forgot to give my offering and that she was taking it. Regardless, many additional offers were given in recompence on those occasions to uphold right relations. If you find yourself in a similar situation, making offers in recompense would be a good idea. Offerings of value, perhaps more significant than your usual offerings, would be appropriate.

When Dedications End

Since many oaths are ones that involve being dedicated to a deity, it is important to understand that even when you uphold your oaths, they may still end. Oaths have to be accepted by the gods and can be broken when the gods deem it so. The gods are real, with agency, their own agendas, and their own goals. You could do everything right, be dedicated to a deity for years and then have that relationship change through no real fault of your own. Not everything is permanent.

Many of us who feel they were called by a deity often assume that said deity will be a permanent fixture in our lives and spiritual work. In many cases this is true, but not always. Even when we share oaths and vows of service or dedication to a deity, there is no guarantee of a relationship being permanent. Sometimes certain deities will play a big part in your life for certain times. That could last a few years or decades. Sometimes this end of relationship might be a slow process, and other times it can be sudden when the deity makes it clear the relationship will be changing.

Often a dedication ending has to do with a person taking on new or different spiritual work. Other times it is because we haven't been fulfilling our agreements with deity and they essentially have withdrawn. I think it is important to understand that dedications are a two-way street. Like any relationship, whether it be a romantic one or a friendship, both parties have agency and have to willingly choose to continue the relationship, to feed it and make it grow. Just like people in our everyday lives, sometimes you grow apart. Sometimes the goals you have don't line up with the other person's anymore. The things that brought you together and cemented that connection might not be there anymore. This happens in divine relationships too. Perhaps the most easily recognizable example is when someone leaves one religion for another. Like many folks who find Paganism I was baptized and went through different religious dedications within Christianity. I wasn't exactly raised Christian. I was a teenager and already learning Witchcraft before my parents felt the need to bring my brother and me to church. In general, we were raised being told that whatever religion we chose would be up to us. When it became pretty clear that choice wasn't going to be Christianity, for me that turned into we could chose when we left home but in the meantime we were going to be exposed to my parents version of religion, like it or not. But the rituals I took part in connected me to the god of Christianity, a god I later would part ways with amicably in favor of other gods who called to my spirit. Although undergoing those rituals were not my idea or even really my choice, it was still an ending of a relationship with a divine being. Most Pagans who have left behind Christianity for Paganism have also ended such a divine dedication in favor of another one.

Endings don't have to be bad. Many times, they are healthy and necessary. It's ok to mourn these changes and take times to reflect on how a deity's influence in your life changed you. It also doesn't mean you have to stop worshiping that deity. You may no longer have a dedication to them but most likely still know them very well and depending on what tradition you are a part of will more than likely still on occasion honor them or make offerings to them. What changes is how much your life is entwined with them. Not unlike seeing a friend who might have moved away, and you lost touch with.

Acknowledging the end of a dedication is important. How you wish to do that may depend on the deity. It might be done ritualistically; it might be done through making an offering of great significance to represent the gratitude and thanks you have for that deity's influence in your life. However you chose to recognize this kind of change, if you find yourself in this place, what is done or offered should be of appropriate value and done with reverence.

Elements of an Oath

Regardless of what kind of oath, promise, or bargain you make with the gods many of the elements will be the same. Each is important to think through thoroughly before committing to the oath.

Time Frame

This is very key to being able to fulfill your oath. Leaving things open ended is not always a good idea. Keep in mind that an oath can be renewed. So, setting a period of time to it doesn't mean that you can't renew it at some point. These tend to be more important to oaths of reciprocity than other oaths but should still be considered regardless. Think through all the ramifications and possible issues related to the time frame you are outlining.

Specifics of What Is Promised

The key here is to be clear and specific. Pretend you are making a wish with a genie who might misinterpret what you say. Words have power and the wording of your oath will shape your reality after you make it. You may also wish to add in things that you aren't willing to do as well as things you are willing to do. If you are offering an oath of priesthood, then that requires you to spend a lot of time thinking about what priesthood means to you. Certain terminology does not always have the same meanings to different people. If you are offering your service, well, what does service mean? Are there limits to that service? Does it include regularly doing XYZ? Again, take time to consider meanings. If you don't know what you are offering, then deity may decide to put their own meaning to your words. You don't necessarily have to spell it out in the actual wording on your oath, but as long as you have a firm understanding of what it is you are offering with those words it is enough to lock it into the energy and DNA of your oath.

Surety

This may or may not be present in an oath. It's like saying "cross your heart and hope to die if you lie." It is your assurance that your word will be fulfilled, or you welcome some kind of punishment or ill luck to befall you in compensation. It is also verbally acknowledging that there are consequences to you not fulfilling your end of the bargain. That isn't to say there will not be consequences if you don't add this part to your oath, but just don't be surprised if you get what you ask for. It might be something specific offered as a penalty, or something nonphysical like luck or your connection to deity, like saying, "may the sky fall on me or the earth swallow me if I am untrue to my word." Oaths taken on swords where the wielder says if they should break their oath that the sword would turn against them in battle or break would be an example.

Witnesses

Your mileage will vary on this one depending on the tradition you are part of. In some traditions those who witness your oath are as responsible as you are for fulfilling the oath that is made. They are there to witness the oath and on some level validate that it was spoken and must be adhered to. In some traditions if you are failing to keep your word or need aid in keeping your word, those who witnessed the oath are obligated to help you fulfill it in whatever way they can. The blowback for not doing this is less so for the witness, but it is generally looked very poorly upon if a witness could have aided the oath taker and did not offer their aid. But again, this may vary depending on the tradition in question. Culturally it is the idea that our obligations to the gods are shared as a community, and that your spiritual welfare can impact my own spiritual welfare. If you are having someone witness your oath, the implications of why they are acting as a witness should be discussed beforehand and understood by all witnessing the oath.

Suggested Exercises

1. Examine your own oaths and contracts with deity. What category do they fall within?

2. Spend some time journaling how your oaths and vows have changed your spiritual work. How have they changed you?

CHAPTER EIGHT

Patron Deities &
Other Divine Relationships

We are about to leave for a trip. It is part vacation, part pilgrimage to visit sacred sites. Preparing to go on a trip isn't just packing my suitcase. Before we leave there are offerings to be made, offerings to the deities that have a special place in my home and heart. Offerings are made at all the household altars. Many of these deities aren't traditionally associated with travel, but they are the deities I worship, and I feel that we bring our deities wherever we go. These are the beings that I served and that watch out for me. So, when I'll be traveling, overseeing, and seeking a spiritual retreat, it is only appropriate for me to honor them before I go.

I move from altar to altar, leaving offerings, speaking quietly, asking for safe travels and asking that our home be protected while we are away. At many of the altars I feel a warm energy of recognition and connection. My words are heard, my offerings accepted. This continues as I make my way through the house.

When I come to the small wall niche that is home to my altar to Oya, I pour her an offering and leave pieces of dark chocolate in the offering bowl. I reach out with my mind and speak to Oya, praising her. I see the powerful winds and storms she rules over and imagine them turning into calm breezes and clear skies. It's hurricane season where we live, and it has been in the back of our minds that we could be away while a storm hits. I ask her to quell her storms and watch over our home while we are away. I become aware of her presence and I feel my offering is accepted. But there is more: Oya asks that I do something for her on my journey. The request comes as both words and impressions that flood through me. I must leave her an offering, nine pennies, at the entrance of every graveyard I visit on my trip and she will do as I ask. Oya is the queen of cemeteries, and it is she who guards the boundaries between the living and the dead. I agree and send my thanks to Oya.

When I pack my suitcase I make sure to have a roll of pennies tucked away in one of the little compartments. I do not think there will be many graveyards on our trip, but I know of at least two we will be visiting. So, I decide to be overprepared. I am not part of an African Traditional Religion or group, but Oya has always been a powerful force in my life. She appeared out of nowhere asking me to pass on a message to a friend who was dedicated to her, and then after that she continued to show up. She is a deity that often appears in my dreams and has helped me through dark times. My devotion to her is perhaps not the same as my devotion to the Morrigan, but it is still deep and meaningful. Just as my relationship to different people in my life are each different and unique.

I was perhaps just a little surprised at the number of grave-yards we ended up encountering on our trip. A lot of the sacred sites we visited had a graveyard of some kind on or near the site we were visiting. I was soon running out of pennies and had to dig through my wallet for a few in the end. But I kept my word and Oya kept hers. It was more than just fulfilling a bargain. Each offering at the entrance of the graveyards we came across was a way to honor and keep that connection to Oya strong. There were other gods we were honoring and seeking on this trip, but Oya was there too. I was in a land that really didn't have much connection to her stories, but I was there, and I was and am in some part hers. So, she was there too, because I was there.

I walked away from the last graveyard we came across think-ing that we all have a whole host of gods walking beside and sur-rounding us. The devotional relationships we have become a part of the fiber of our being, and we bring the threads of those rela-tionships with us wherever we go and into everything we do in one way or another.

One of the main purposes of religion or spirituality is to help us understand our place in the universe, and what our relationship is to divinity. The gods are vast beings; in many ways it might be more accurate to think of them as forces of nature or the universe. No matter how much we try there will always be aspects of the divine that are beyond knowing in our incarnated state. Fully conceptualizing the scope of the gods is like trying to hold the ocean in a teacup. The ocean remains vast, but our conscious understanding of it may only be the waters we catch in our teacup. Some of us may scoop up different-tasting waters in our cups. So perhaps it is no wonder that there are many different models for devotional relationships. Some are permanent, some are not. Before we look at how to navigate some of these relationships, let's first look at several types of dedications and how they differ.

Patron Deity

Patron means a person who gives financial or other kinds of support to a person or group. We tend to think of famous painters and artists of the past being supported by wealthy patrons. Similarly, a patron deity lends you support in a spiritual sense. In Paganism this term is used in many ways and may have different meanings within a given tradition. In general, a patron deity is a modern term used for a god/goddess that you have a deep connection to, and usually a formal dedication to. The term could be extended to other beings, for example if one adopted a Christian saint as a patron, or those who have a patron relationship with Faery Queens or other powerful or semi-divine beings. Again, there tends to be a sliding scale of what we each consider divine. Regardless, the dedication, oath, or personal relationship you have with a patron deity makes the connection more profound than other deities you might worship.

Patron deities may also be adopted when one is initiating into certain traditions. A coven or group may have certain gods belonging to that tradition, and becoming part of that group may require making oaths of service to those gods. Similarly, in many Afro-Caribbean religions once an initiate is ready to become a full member of the religion, a priest will throw cowrie shells or perform other divinations to determine what deity "crowns" that person, ultimately becoming their patron deity.

I view the gods as very real beings with their own personalities. Every deity operates differently. Gods have their own agendas, and to some degree I think that influences who they choose to court as worshipers and dedicants. In my own experience, very often the gods come looking for you rather than it being the other way around. They may be around in our lives for quite a while before we even notice it. I suspect that once we make a habit of opening ourselves to the divine and the realm of spirits, our receptiveness to such interactions is taken note of.

Fulltrui

This is a term specific to Heathenry, or those who worship the Norse pantheon of gods. *Fulltrui* (for a male deity) and *fulltrua* (for a goddess) means "trusted friend" and in general is used to describe a deity one has a dedication to or feels especially close to. Like having a patron deity, it in no way means that one's fulltrui is the only deity one can worship. The main difference I see with this concept vs. the Neo-Pagan patron deity is that this kind of relationship is seen as less commonplace. Heathens are not required to have a fulltrui, but some Heathens look down on the concept.

It is debatable if this practice has more modern roots or if it has historical significance. There is some evidence of this practice in the Sagas, people who were called the "beloved friend" of a deity, and in some cases took part of a god's name as their own to acknowledge their closeness to that deity. This wasn't always so beneficial to the person who had the close connection to the deity. Those who were god-friends with Odin tended to die in battle. In the *Gisla's Saga* Thorgrim Freysgothi was so loved by Frey that the god honored him by preventing snow from covering his grave. He is certainly given favor by Frey, but he still dies.

In general, those who have a fulltrui see the relationship as a special connection where their focus in offerings or ritual may be more centered on that deity. Other deities are still honored. The special connection isn't necessarily one of service or servitude, which many connect to the relationship one has with a patron deity. In some cases, this relationship is formally done with an oath, while others see it as a relationship that forms over time like any mundane friendship.

God-Spouse

Most of us are familiar with this type of dedication in the context of Christianity where nuns become the "brides" of the Christian god. Although less common within modern Paganism there are those who relate to their relationship with the gods as a spousal one. This kind of dedication might be marked with a ceremony or oath like any of the other relationships we have looked at.

In general, this is the hardest relationship to describe because most Pagans who consider themselves a god-spouse see it as a deeply personal and very private relationship. Some see it as a connection with deity that is all-consuming. Others view its intensity as one where the spouse becomes a window for deity to experience the physical world. In one case a person I know who is a god-spouse feels the conception of their children was in some way influenced or initiated by a deity. There is a kind of possessiveness to this kind of connection, and often those who feel they are the spouse of a certain god will not choose to work with others who share the same kind of all-consuming relationship with that deity. Like all the relationships we are looking at, it varies from person to person.

Contracts & Bargains

We don't usually think of these as a type of dedication, but in many cases they are. These kinds of relationships have specific end dates and terms. Usually it is when someone offers their service to a deity for, say, a year and a day, or until a certain task is accomplished. Sometimes the terms of such contracts are renewable, or one can choose to make them permanent. In general, the wording of such contracts and bargains are of the upmost importance.

In some cases, there may not even be an element of worship to contracts of this nature, and they are all business and less personal relationship. It can be seen as negotiating with an outside contractor on a project. Medieval occult manuscripts that talk about summoning angels, demons, and other spirits would be along these lines. The spirit is usually summons for a specific purpose or to help the magician achieve a specific task. Eliciting the spirits again might be coerced by some magical means or negotiation might occur. Regardless, all these kinds of agreements revolve around service or actions rendered by both parties. I will give you this if you do this for me, etc.

Dedications can vary widely from one dedicant to another. Our relationships with the gods are unique because we are not cookie-cutter copies of one another. The gods themselves come in many different temperaments and varieties. The important thing to keep in mind is that your dedication is between you and the divine. The oaths I have spoken will not be the same as your own. We all have different work to do in the world, we all need different things. The types of devotional relationships we have looked at here may resemble what you experience or may not. Every relationship, divine or otherwise, is different.

Suggested Exercises

1. Examine some of the relationships you have had with different deities and spirits. What categories do they fall in?

2. Think about the kind of relationship you wish to foster with deity. Try to be mindful of your intentions as you go through your devotional practices with deity.

3. Consider how your relationships with deities have changed. Have your relationships with the divine started as one type then evolved into something else?

A Ritual of Dedication

You Will Need

A meaningful offering

An oath prewritten

Divination tool of your choice

This ritual case can be used as is or tailored to your needs and specific practices. It is just an example of how you can approach making a formal oath of dedication to a deity. This of course will require a lot of forethought before the ritual itself. Deciding what kind of oath or vow you are offering to deity and its specific nature and wording will be key. This should be something you spend time crafting and consulting with deity about before the ritual. You will also need a meaningful offering to give to deity along with your oath. This should be something significant and personal in nature, something that both the deity likes as well as something that is connected to your own personal relationship with deity. It doesn't have to be expensive or excessive, just meaningful.

A week prior to the ritual you should spend some time doing additional devotional work, connecting with deity and general purification. If possible, memorize the words of your oath; otherwise have it written down. If you are working indoors make sure there is a bowl or appropriate place to leave your offering in your ritual space. You might choose to do this as a full ritual, in whatever tradition or manner you prefer, or you could also do this in front of your altar or sacred space.

When you are ready prepare the space in whatever manner you chose. Spend a few moments connecting to deity. This might be done by saying a prayer, chanting, or some light journey work. When you feel the presence of deity, say:

I honor you, (name of deity)
I am your devotee,
I have sung your name, and praised your deeds and powers
You have been at my side a (protector / teacher, etc., name your
relationship with them)
I come to you to offer my devotion and oaths
May you accept what I offer

When you are ready, say your oath of dedication that you have written ahead of time. When you are done, place your offering in your offering bowl. Depending on the offering if you are outside it might be appropriate to offer it to a fire or bury it, etc. Say:

(Name of deity), *I give you this offering in gratitude*
May you accept this offering and my vow!

When you are ready, take your preferred divination tool and use it to determine if the offering and oath was accepted. Spend a few more moments opening your awareness to deity and see if there are any messages they wish to impart to you.

Close the ritual in whatever manner you chose.

PART THREE

Priest

Priest. Priestess. These are words that invoke images of ancient ceremonies, of sibyls proclaiming prophecies in oracular caves, of Druids making offerings to the gods in mossy forest groves. We imagine these figures as vessels for the gods to speak through, being wise and profound for their connections to the unseen worlds. Unfortunately, the reality of serving as a priest is far less glamorous, and usually involves inconvenient godly problems, being the first one to an event to set up and the last one to leave so you can vacuum up and clean up what's left of the pot luck items and pay the bill on the rental space. It can be deeply profound and rewarding work, but if you begin down the path of priesthood assuming its glamorous, assuming it's all about you, well than you'll be in for a rude awakening. I don't say this to discourage you. In this section you will find information I very much wished I would have known when I first entered into the service to my gods as a priestess. But I can say I started down that path with the naive belief that the longer one was on a spiritual path, the easier the work became. Once I had the foundation I needed, everything would just get easier! Wrong. The longer you do the work, the harder it becomes. Yes, you will be more equipped to handle it, but it doesn't get easier. If anything, the work becomes harder because your skill level has increased. Above all being a priest or priestess is to be in service to others, your gods chiefly and potentially to your community, no matter how large or small that may be. That means there are a whole host of expectations laid at your feet and not all of these are from the gods.

Navigating the landscape of being a priest is a daunting task, but a rewarding one in the end. Now that we have looked at how our personal relationships with the divine can evolve we will explore what it means for that relationship to include the community, when your relationship to the divine become a bridge for others to find connection and meaning. How does one serve the gods in this capacity? How does one balance serving the needs of the community alongside the needs of the gods, and one's personal relationship with the divine? How do we avoid burnout? These are all important things to consider when walking the path of the priest. While all the other types of devotion we have looked at thus far center primarily on your person relationship with deity, the realm of priesthood is all about facilitating that experience for others. It is the most demanding kind of devotion, and the most binding relationship we can have with the gods.

CHAPTER NINE

What Is a Priest?

*I place the torc on the altar. It is one that I have made. To me it is
something symbolic of a queen, and I am honoring and holding
space for a Witch Queen. I think of an almost identical torc that
she wore often around her neck, also made by my hand. The tears
come as I place the candle, bright red like her hair, within the circle of the torc. A crow feather. Several crystals for peace, comfort,
strength. Then a single rough ruby. I think of the line of a song
about the souls that the Morrigan likes best, that they are rubies
in the raven's nest. My friend is one of those rubies, and she is
dying. She is too young, too full of life. I thought there would be
more time, more memories to make, but there isn't. Everything
that could be done, has been done. They are taking her off life
support, and all I can do, all anyone can do, is hold space for her.
Be a comfort to her, a light to guide her way. To hold space for her
and surround her with our love.*

*It breaks my heart that I can't be there to hold her hand, to tell
her "I love you" one more time, to see her smile just once more. I
need my gods right now. I need to hear their voices because I will*

never hear my friend's voice again. So as the tears flow and the candle is lit, I call to them. I call to the goddess we both loved and served, I call to all the other gods she worshiped. I call to them to guide her home. To weave peace and love and comfort around her. To sooth her passage home, to them. I am not the only one who is doing this. There are other candles lit and other prayers being said. I try to see all the energy we are sending come together like clasped hands around a circle. I feel the Morrigan's wings wrap around me as I weep. I feel the presence of other gods too, coming to my call. Shining, towering figures surrounding my friend in their presence.

Being a priestess means you are a bridge. Sometimes that bridge is about helping others connect to the gods, to feel their presence. Many times that is done in ritual, or as an oracle, or a counselor. There are baby blessings, and initiations, and then there is this. There is being the bridge at the end of our travels. I feel the weight of it today. Being a priest or priestess means you are not just in service to the gods; you are in service to the community. You are the midwife of spiritual experience and sometimes the midwife of the soul to the Otherworlds.

I say many things as I watch the candle flame and hold space. I falter on the last line. "Fly free, my friend." And soon, she does.

I think when one decides to take up the mantle of priesthood you really have to consider what that title means to you. There are many words and terms one might use as a priest: Priest, Priestess, Druid, Gothi, Babalawo, just to name a few. In many cases some of these titles have several layers of meaning, and one might adopt such a title with one meaning in mind, while tossing out the rest.

It is easy to see where arguments over who can and can't use a term, as well as what that title even means, in regard to one's connection to deity, can arise. Druid is a historical title used to describe the priestly caste of several Pan-Celtic cultures. Today Druid can refer only to the spiritual path one is on or indicate that one serves as a priest within their tradition. If you asked a modern practitioner what being a Druid means to them, likely you would get different answers across different traditions, and various additional meanings from one person to the next. Similarly, Bean Feasa, which means "wise woman" in Irish, has several layers of meaning and can be a term used to describe a Witch, a female practitioner of magic, a prophetess or seeress, or a Faery Doctor. Faery Doctor is itself a term used in the past to simply describe a connection and affinity to the Otherworlds and the faery folk, regardless of one's religious convictions. Yet I have also seen an upsurge of modern folks using it as a term to describe their service as a type of priest of the Faery Folk. Additionally, someone who is a priest or priestess in a traditional Wiccan coven might have vastly different priestly roles within their groups than someone who is a priest of another Pagan tradition yet uses the exact same terminology to describe themselves. Furthermore, some might prefer to use modern terminology, while others may choose to reclaim words from specific cultures to describe their roles within priesthood. Are we all talking about the same thing, just using different words? Or are there fundamental differences in the many terms one could use to describe their flavor of priesthood?

The problem is the function of every priest will be slightly different for everyone, both because of the different gods we serve and the traditions we follow. Being a priest of the Morrigan will not be the same kind of experience as being a priest of Lugh or Freya. How the god or gods you serve influence your life will be different. The roles of a priest also will differ depending on the group you work with or the concept of priesthood within a given cultural practice or tradition. An eclectic practitioner will approach things differently than one who is a priest within a Wiccan initiatory tradition, or one who practices Irish Polytheism or Heathenry. Also, on an individual level you may find your ideas about being a priest or priestess will diverge from what another person believes who follows the same path. Despite our many different approaches, there are still commonalities.

In many ways we try to model Pagan priesthood after what we have been exposed to in mainstream religions like Christianity. Their priests wear many hats, and to those hats we add a few extra mystical ones. In Paganism we generally expect our priests to be counselors, ritualists, magicians, seers, teachers, event organizers, community builders, and mediators between the unseen and humanity. Most of these roles focus on the wider community. Community can be an important part of the work of a priest, but there are other models. If we look to the ancient world, we find priesthood looked a little different. Temples across the ancient world were literally the houses of the gods. They were places people came to pay their respects and worship the gods, but it was less the gathering place of the community than a modern Church is. The function of the ancient priest was to tend to the needs of the gods, to make sacrifice and keep right relations with the gods. In many cases in the ancient world the common people would not be admitted into temples, or particularly sacred parts of the temple. In modern times we can see this in Buddhism, where parts of the temples are to house sacred objects, usually in a stupa, that are not accessible to the public. The point is they upheld the rites of the gods and made offerings to them, but whether the public was part of that didn't always matter. One can serve as a priest to the gods and not necessarily serve the community as part of that commitment.

If you serve as a priest to other spirits, such as the sidhe, then your devotion may have nothing to do with the community of humanity at all. Morgan Daimler describes this in reference to her own devotion as a priestess of the Daoine Maithe, or Good Neighbors. "There's also a pervasive sense that the clergy person may be serving the Gods or spirits but is primarily serving the human community and in place to aid that human community and to help it grow and flourish in its spirituality. I am not part of that kind of priesthood, although clergy I certainly am … Now it is true that people do contact me for guidance about problems relating to the Good Neighbors, but in this context I am not advocating for or trying to assist the humans—I'm on the side of the Other."[2]

So where does that leave us? Well, it does require one to take some time to decide what the term priest/ess means to you individually. If you are using different terminology, then you should do research on the title you choose to take up. What did it mean historically and through different time periods? Why do you feel this is the correct title to use for yourself? Sometimes it may be a title given to you within your community, or your faith, or one a deity places on you. Regardless, understanding the connotations of the term and taking time to work out your own definition of a

---

2. Morgan Daimler, "Priesthood in Service to the Other—Part 1: The Wide View" Living Liminally (blog), May 10, 2019 https://lairbhan.blogspot.com/2019/05/priesthood-in-service-to-other.html.

priest is important. Even if you are taking on priesthood as part of an initiatory path where the role and definition of a priest is well mapped out, it is still important to decide what that means to you on an individual level.

Additionally, one needs to consider what offering your service as a priest to deity will entail. How will being a priest change your devotion to your gods? Will it include service to the community? If so, in what way? What will the title you take to describe your priesthood be and what does it mean in the context of your devotion? Sorting through your thoughts and ideas through journaling would be a good start. Write your own definition for a priest or whatever word you decide to use. You can keep what you wrote next to your altar or in your sacred space as a reminder of what this kind of service means to you. Spend time speaking to your gods about what they will require of you as a priest. Negotiate and understand what you are promising them when you make the choice to offer this kind of service to the gods.

It's also important to consider that some of this isn't up to you. In my personal opinion the gods make the priest. They have to accept the service you are offering, and no one can force them to. Offering to serve the divine isn't something once said you can back out of. It is a lifelong commitment, and it involves not only giving up some free will but also a great deal of time in service to the deity you are binding yourself to. It is not a calling everyone should take up or is ready for.

Not everyone's version of priesthood will be the same, but there are some common traits that apply to most priests regardless of what tradition one follows or the terminology one uses.

Maintaining Right Relations

Maintaining right relations with the gods can come in many forms. When a devotee makes regular offerings they are doing this. They are honoring the gods and building an energetic connection between themselves and the divine. This remains very much the same when one takes on the mantle of priesthood. After all, the reason they may seek out the aid of a priest is because they have a strong connection to deity, and like any bond it must be continually fostered. But there is also an additional element to this with priesthood. Many times, as a priestess I often step in to makes sure right relations continue between the gods and the community. For example, several years ago I was at a public Lammas ritual where Ra and Selene where invoked. The majority of the ritual has nothing to do with them, other than that they were the god and goddess the person running the ritual has decided to invoke. The thing was that the person invoking them did a good job; their presence was very palpable to me. They were there, and they were promptly forgotten after being invoked. The ritual continued focusing on the theme of Lammas, and they were never even thanked or bid farewell to. By the end of the ritual the energy was not pleasant. There was an air of annoyance. It was like they were saying: "You called to us, we showed up! Why are we being ignored?" I wasn't the only one who noticed it, and after the circle was opened and the ritual ended two others and I quickly walked to a quiet area to make things right. We poured offerings and left food, offered praise and in the style of the ritual used bid them farewell. The energy settled after that. The three of us weren't leading the ritual; one could argue it wasn't our godly or energetic mess to clean up. Yet, as a priest you are the bridge between the divine and humanity. Even if it wasn't our mess to clean up, it was our obligation as priests to maintain good relations with the gods, to fix the misstep of others.

Maintaining this right relation with the divine could also come in the form of hosting public rituals or seasonal celebrations where you help others foster a relationship with deity. Or it can be just being in the right place at the right time to handle a godly situation when it arises.

Maintaining the Lore and Traditions

This will probably be the function we are the most familiar with. The priest is someone who know the stories of the gods and recounts them to the people. Whether it be reading a verse from the Bible or recounting the stories of Odin, or the Druids memorizing the genealogies of gods and kings, the concept is the same. The priest passes down the lore and stories of the gods, often using them as teaching tools.

Just as the stories of the gods provide a shared foundation within a group or tradition, the rituals one shares with a group also maintain the traditions of that faith. These would be rituals of coming of age, a baby blessing, seasonal rites, an initiation into a tradition, funerary rites. These are the rituals that all who are part of that group may have undergone at some point. In traditional Wicca you could see these as the initiatory processes of attaining all three degrees. In more eclectic Pagan circles this could be a priest/ess holding the seasonal rites and passing on the meanings behind each Sabbat to the group. These rites form the spiritual foundation of the community and give a sense of shared experience. If I recount a particularly moving Imbolc ritual to you, you more than likely think of an Imbolc ritual you have been a part of and thus we have commonality of spiritual experience that would not be possible without a priest facilitating such rituals.

Bridge Between the People and the Gods

This is perhaps the most important function of a priest. Whether it is through rituals one leads, through their writing on a deity, or serving as oracle or channel for deity to speak through them, a priest is a conduit for the divine. Your connection to deity will help others experience the gods, and build their own connection to them, through your facilitation. The priest is the one who knows the rituals, knows the rites and offerings to make to please the gods. They already have that thread of connection to the unseen and can draw on it so others can experience their presence. You might also be asked to offer prayers and sacrifices to the gods on the behalf of others. This also means the priest is the one who facilitates this connection between the gods and others during initiations and rites of passage. This can be anything from a baby blessing to burial rites.

Beseeches the Gods
on Behalf of the Community

I have seen it argued that the difference between a shaman and a priest is that the priest is the bridge between the people and the gods while the shaman is one who contends with the gods and spirits. The shaman is a lawyer of sorts dealing with good and bad spiritual beings, reminding the gods of their promises to the people and battling spirits that are harmful to the community's wellbeing. I would say that a Pagan priest is in many ways a blend of the two. The Pagan priest is a bridge between the unseen and the community and upholds the rites of the gods, but they also are the one others go to with spiritual problems akin to the ones a shaman traditionally handles. A priest might exorcise ill spirits or bless a house, as well as do a baby blessing. A priest is also one who might beseech the gods for aid on behalf of a community member or might reveal information through trance in order to counsel or restore right relations with the gods. Perhaps this overlap of functions is because most forms of Paganism include the practice of magic and trance work.

Counseling or advice Giving

Counseling and giving advice can take many forms for a priest. Usually this revolves around how to connect with deity or helping others process their experience with deity. A priest has a stronger connection to the gods they serve; thus, others will come to you for insight in their own relationships with the divine. Other advice might be dealing with angry spirits or how to appease the gods when there are missteps. Life advice, whether that be how to live a good life, marriage counseling, or general life coaching, also falls into the realm of the priest.

I feel in general most Pagan priests will feel equipped to handle advice about spiritual practice and the nature of the gods. That is something a priest has ample experience in. Other kinds of guidance you might not be equipped or trained for. Clergy in other religions usually receive training in these areas. Seeking out classes, books on the subject, or other resources that can help you navigate counseling those going through crisis and other life issues would be invaluable. If it is not something you are comfortable with, or something you don't have the training in, it is better to suggest that the person seek professional help. You can still support them through the process and act as spiritual support by helping them find professional help they are comfortable with.

Have Been Dedicated to Their Gods for a Long Time

I add this qualification because I all too often see folks who are newly Pagan or just discovered a deity who after having a vivid encounter with a god suddenly feel they are meant to be a priest of that deity. Now that may be true. Maybe that deity does eventually want you to serve as their priest. But becoming a priest takes years. You must spend time as a devotee and dedicant to a deity to truly understand them. Connecting to and understanding a deity can take years. You can't skip the steps and you shouldn't seek out priesthood until you are fully grounded in a deep understanding of the god you serve and the path or tradition you practice. And honestly someone who had a profound experience with a deity can be someone on a different path. Vivid meaningful experiences don't just happen to priests; they can happen to anyone.

If you were working through a traditional degree system, it would likely take you several years before you reached the level of a priest. Initiatory traditions are in the minority at this point in Paganism, but we need to stop and think about why that process took a great deal of time. Why is someone who just joined an initiatory path not instantly a priest? Well, because they haven't taken the time to hone their skills, and to learn the skills. Outside of initiatory traditions, this should be no different.

Suggested Exercises

1. Spend time journaling about what being a priest means to you.

2. What word or title describes your priesthood? Why have you chosen to use this word/title in relation to your work?

3. Create a statement of purpose describing your work as a priest. This is something good to come back to and reassess every so often. Evaluate if anything has changed. Are there new layers to the work you do that you have realized now vs. when you wrote your statement of purpose?

4. Which of the different roles of a priest touched on do you fit into? Are there other roles you wish to take on as a part of priesthood? What tools or training do you need to be able to incorporate these roles?

CHAPTER TEN

Service to the Gods

The battlefield looks more like a nature preserve than a grave-yard. We walk around the visitor center; there are diagrams and a short video with reenactors playing various parts. After the video we walk around what is now Dade Battlefield Park. There are benches and picnic tables in certain areas. There are also paths through the trees dotted with various monuments, and stone pillars with plaques recounting where different people fell during the battle fought here. There are offerings in my bag. We haven't come here for a picnic. The Morrigan has asked me to start visiting battlefields. It seems like an odd request at first. During my daily devotions I asked her, "How can I honor you?" and her answer was "Go to the battlefields." The rest was more a feeling than words. "Speak my words, bring peace, bring rest." It will be an ongoing practice I will continue to do. But this is my first visit to a battlefield for this purpose, and I'm still sorting out exactly what she wants me to do.

Serving the gods can take many forms. Sometimes it is hosting ritual, talking to others about a god you serve to help them on their own path; other times the gods will ask you to do things. While I walk around and read the plaques, I think about what the Morrigan wants. The energy of the land here feels wrong. I feel eyes watching me; everything feels unsettled and unfriendly. "Speak my words," she tells me. So, I find a place out of the way of others enjoying the park. I note that most people seem to avoid the area I have wandered into. I pull out the offerings of tobacco and whiskey. I spend some time connecting to the land, to the spirits I feel watching. I make my offerings. I say the words of the Morrigan's peace prophecy. I reach out to the spirits I feel are bound, stuck perhaps, to this place. I tell them that they can move on, that they are remembered, and their sacrifices are recognized. I stay there for a long while. But when I am done the place feels lighter. The energy is not hostile anymore. I feel as if some spirits moved on; not all, but some. At the very least they are more settled. They have been remembered and offered respect in the place that they fell. This is something I will do many times after this. But I would never have started doing this work if I hadn't been a priestess of the Morrigan, if I hadn't listened to how she wanted me to be in service to her. Sometimes our service to the gods will be things we expect; other times they are making offerings to the dead at old almost forgotten battlefields.

We have looked at some of the things that define priesthood, but most of these have been things that priests do, roles they take on in their service to the gods. Those are certainly important in understanding what priesthood is and if you wish to take that step in your devotion. But there is also the personal side of priesthood, your personal relationship with the gods you serve. Much of this book has been about how to connect with the gods, how to hear their voices and build relationships with them. Priesthood is just another relationship, but it's a complicated one because it opens your devotion and dedication to the gods to others in the community. It's a little bit like being in an open relationship: you have multiple needs and expectations to manage, but you also have to nourish the individual relationships and feed them, so they stay strong. You will have the needs of the community calling for your attention, but then you will also have the needs of the gods to attend to, as well as your personal relationship to them to nurture. It's a bit of a juggling act. Even if your priesthood is focused primarily on the needs of the gods and doesn't really involve the wider community, your oath of service to the gods can still be life altering because the gods will expect more from you. The relationship is still changed by your oath, and like any oath it will be expected to be fulfilled. So, let's take some time to look at the personal side of priesthood. On an individual level how will it change our relationships to the gods? What does being in service to the gods really mean for the priest's own spiritual journey?

In my experience the gods can ask all sorts of things of their priests. Sometimes these things seem simple. Maybe it is just being in the right place to help someone. Maybe it is bettering yourself, so you are healthier, happier, and more able to serve them fully in the future. Maybe it is starting an event in their honor or writing a book. Maybe it is putting in that extra hour of practice refining a skillset. These things can seem minor, but the gods are looking at things from a much wider perspective than we are. I have been asked by the Morrigan to make offerings to the dead at a battlefield. It is a private practice, a service to her I offer because she asked me to do so. No one would really know that I do this if I didn't talk about it. It is not a service to the community; instead it is a service to her and the spirits of the battlefield. Other times the lines blur. I often find I am nudged to be in the right place at the right time to talk to someone who needs support for whatever reason. On the one hand this is a service to others, but on the other it is something I feel directed by the Morrigan to do and in many ways is a direct service to her. For example, during an event I run I had been turning in for the night when I had an odd feeling that I needed to be somewhere. I felt a clear direction from the Morrigan to just go walking around the area we were camped in. So, I walked around the camp, and nothing happened. Eventually I needed to use the bathroom, so I headed in that direction. On my way someone came out of the building we were using as a temple space in tears. I went up to them and we ended up having a long conversation. Little nudges like that can be part of priesthood, they can be part of your service to the divine. They are the things most people won't see you do, but they need doing regardless.

Cleaning and tending sacred sites when on pilgrimage or the sites I claim as sacred where I live is another act of service. Very often sites that are frequently visited accumulate a lot of garbage. That can include the things that have been left as offerings. Cleaning and tending those sites are an act of service to the divine. It is not unlike temple tending, just on a larger scale.

Part of my service to Brigid is flame tending. Like making offers to the spirits of the battlefield, this is something not done in public usually. It is a service to Brigid that she has asked me to do. Similarly, I know a friend whose service to the gods is tending an ancestor altar and making offerings to the dead each night. I have seen several people take up a similar practice in the wake of the Covid-19 pandemic, spending time honoring the newly dead and easing their passage as well as honoring the ancestors. These are all practices that could be done with the community but very often are quiet personal services to the divine. They are not really done for the community, which is part of what makes them distinct from the other activities of a priest. It instead focuses on the spirit world.

Part of being in service to the gods is also retaining a strong connection to them. It is easy to become overwhelmed with service to the community. There is so much work to be done, that we forget as a priest we still must maintain our own personal connections to deity. Many of the practices we have already looked at in part one can be excellent tools to help a priest continue to deepen their connection to deity. Remember it's not leveling up; even a priest needs to be continually refining their devotional practices. After all, if you lose that connection to deity, there is little point in being a priest of that deity. Service to the gods, when contrasted with service to the community, can be an incredibly quiet and private thing. It can be temple tending, and making offerings, and building that deep connection to the divine, so that when they call you to do something you are attuned enough to hear it.

What are We Giving Up?

I think a lot of time people focus on what they are gaining from taking on the title of priest or priestess. There is a certain amount of authority that comes with these titles in the wider community and within groups. It says you have reached a certain level of study, or that you have a very intense relationship with a god. You are the one to go to for answers about a particular deity, or tradition, because you have been there and done that. You have the personal experience or insight that others may not have. We forget that there are things we give up as a priest, and I don't just mean the time and energy sacrificed to do many of the things a priest does.

I was vending at a festival once and someone had been directed to me because they were a devotee of the Morrigan. We talked awhile about our own experiences, and then we came to the topic of priesthood. This person had a strong devotion to the Morrigan, clearly one that meant a great deal to them, but they were very firm in their conviction that they didn't want to be a priest of the Morrigan. I found that interesting since most people view being a priest as leveling up or adding a notch to their belt. The reason they gave was that they would be giving up part of their freedom and that wasn't a step they were ready to take, or possibly ever willing to take. It's true, binding yourself to a deity, being in service to them as a priest, does mean giving something up. On some level you are giving up a piece of your free will. It doesn't mean you can't say no or can't negotiate about certain things. You should never do anything you feel is harmful or immoral because you feel deity told you to do so. Generally speaking, I don't find that the gods ask us to do those sorts of things anyway. But it does mean you are in service to something greater. You aren't the one in charge.

Oaths can change our relationships with the gods. Priesthood is a role that often starts with an oath, a vow, a covenant if you will, of service one enters into with the divine. If you are becoming a priest of a particular tradition, by doing so you may be making oaths to a community as well as the gods associated with that tradition. An oath of service to a deity in general means you are giving up some personal freedom in order to gain protections, blessings, and a deeper insight or connection to that deity. There is a give and a take. Sometimes the things the gods ask for might not be what you expect. Taking on the role of a priest may change many things in your own life as well, especially if it comes with certain spiritual prohibitions as part of the oath of service you take. There may be certain things you can't eat anymore, can't wear, or do anymore as a part of the bargain. It is also not a role that you take on only on certain days or for a ritual. The mantle of priesthood should be a part of all aspects of your life, even if it is simply living well and being a good example for others. Just as being a Pagan should be something that is integrated into your everyday life, priesthood is no different.

For myself service to the gods is the most defining quality of a priest. I use the modern terminology of priestess. It is what I feel comfortable with and doesn't carry with it any additional connotations for me that can be misconstrued or muddy the waters as to what I'm using the term to represent. But it is not just being a priestess, it is that I am a priestess of the Morrigan. My personal priesthood is defined by the relationship and connection I specifically have to the Morrigan. Can I serve as a priestess to other gods? Sure, and I often do, for the gods that I feel ask things of me as well as the other gods I have a devotional relationship to. But ultimately my oaths of service are to the Morrigan, and the nature of those oaths are what shape my work as a priestess. If one does not have a connection to the gods, they cannot fulfill the other essential functions of being clergy; they cannot be a bridge between the gods and the community.

What Do You Gain?

Just as you are giving up a portion of free will in becoming a priest, so too do you gain certain things. The more you are connected to a divine being energetically, the more your own energy starts to mirror their own. Their energy starts to become interwoven with your personal energy. This can be said even more so for someone who practices trance possession since they are very literally integrating their persona energy fields with the divine so that they may speak through their bodies. This certainly gives the priest a deeper connection to the deities they serve. It could also instigate a great deal of change in your life as those energies play out and shape your everyday life. What you gain as a priest is to become more attuned and more like the deity you serve. You also get the chance to help build a strong community and help others on their path.

When Is the Right Time to Offer Your Service?

This is something each priest will have to navigate on their own and with their gods. Sometimes the title of priest is something the gods place upon us, and other times the community does before we even take a vow of service. Regardless, what is important is that when you do take an oath or vow as a priest that you understand what you are taking on. Wording, as with any oath, is important. Spend time considering, meditating, doing journey work, to sort out what the terms of your priestwork will be. Write out your oath, consider what the words you have created mean and how they will influence your life and work.

Also be aware that this process doesn't happen overnight. If you just encountered deity and had an intense experience, that doesn't instantly mean you should be a priest to that deity. If your priesthood is centered around a god rather than a tradition, you will likely be both a devotee and dedicant of that god for many years before you take on priesthood. It is also important to remember that there is nothing that says you must be a priest. You can still have a strong relationship with a deity and never serve as their priest.

An Oath Spoken Is Not Always an Oath Accepted

In my personal point of view, it's the gods that make a priest. The gods have to accept your oath. Just speaking a vow doesn't mean the gods will accept it. When such vows are offered it's important to gauge whether or not the vow was accepted by deity. This can be done several ways. You may get a sense of whether or not it was accepted during whatever ritual process you used to offer the oath. If another priest is part of that ritual, they might also have some insight on whether deity accepted what was offered. Divination is perhaps the best method to get a feel for whether or not an oath was accepted. Divination should also be consulted prior to any vows being offered to see if this is the right path to take and what changes might be expected from it.

Suggested Exercises

1. Identify times in your practice when you have been in service to the gods. How have those experiences influenced your path or your relationship to deity?

2. Spend some time journaling or meditating on how you are in service to your gods. What acts of service are meaningful to you and your devotion to deity?

CHAPTER ELEVEN

Service to the Community

The rental contract was signed and paid for several months prior. We have arrived early to set up the altar and string up lights and decorations around the rental hall. As people arrive, we organize where food for the potluck will go. Raffle items get organized on the raffle table. Vendors are directed to pre-assigned marked-out rectangles we have marked out with tape on the floor earlier in the morning. I go over the lines of the ritual in my head as I greet people. I worry that one of the ritual participants with an important part is stuck in traffic and may be late.

When the ritual starts all the worry of the day melts away. I hold the divine within myself. The lines I have memorized flow easily, some I feel the nudge to change as the gods will. Adding something here, taking something out there. The offerings are made. We chant and raise power and at the end I feel energized. I feel the joy of both connecting to the gods and the joy of a ritual that has come together in exactly the way we had hoped. There are lots of hugs. We all share the food everyone has brought and stuff ourselves with vegetarian chili, cookies, and other food offerings.

Then slowly people say their goodbyes. More hugs are exchanged. I send leftover food home with those who I think need it and with those who have been helping through the day. Before I know it, the hall is empty except for a few folks that stay to help clean up and my partner. Offerings are poured reverently outside. A candle has dripped some wax on the floor, and I spend some time carefully removing it. Altar items are packed up and stuffed into the car. I start to realize how tired I am. My partner starts calling for me and I come over to see what is wrong. The toilet is backed up. We quickly search for a plunger and he takes care of the problem. As we turn the lights out and lock the hall, leaving the keys in the designated area we laugh and joke that we have been plunging toilets for the gods today. Because that's the not so glamorous part about being a priest. It means you serve the community, you facilitate rituals, perhaps offer counsel, but you are also the one who cleans up the candle wax and plunges the toilets too.

In many ways our relationships with the gods are the easiest part of priesthood. Our personal devotion and spiritual practices will intensify when we take on the role of clergy and make formal oaths of service to the divine. But when we widen our spiritual practice to the greater community, well, that's when it gets tricky. You aren't just dealing with your own personal expectations, biases and ego; you now are dealing with everyone else's too.

Being a priest doesn't necessarily mean you must have a practice that encompasses the wider community. We can see this in other religions where monks in Eastern faiths dedicate their lives to spiritual study and spend much of their time away from the rest of society tending to a temple or being part of a community of similarly dedicated people. Nuns within Christianity would be another example. While they do participate in some public religious functions, much of their spiritual life is separate from others not on the same path. Within Paganism you could feel called to take up priesthood to a deity and not necessarily make it a public vocation, but rather a private service and devotion to a god.

For myself the public aspects of priesthood were the part I was least prepared for. I'm not very confrontational by nature, and despite my managerial experience in my professional career for some reason I thought in a religious setting people would be on their best behavior. Not always so. I think in part this was because when I was discovering Paganism it was when the AOL running man took five minutes to establish an internet connection, if he established a connection at all. I went to small business occult bookstores to try to meet like-minded people or scoured the listing on Witch-Vox to see if anyone near me identified as Pagan. When I did find people, they usually weren't practicing the same path as myself, but it didn't matter, it was just someone who didn't think what I did was crazy. When you find like-minded people, you tend to believe they are generally good in nature, but even spiritual people can be jerks, or worse, abusers. What did help me was leaning on the training I had been given in managing others in the workplace and adjusting that to managing people in a spiritual community. Other things came with time and experience, with seeing what worked for others, and yet other things came together from training I sought out when I felt I was in over my head.

Your Work as a Priest vs. the Work of the Gods

This is a tricky one, and it took me a while to realize that my work as a priestess and the work of the goddess I served weren't always the same thing. The Morrigan certainly asks me to do certain things and guides me to do work she wants done in the world. But my personal drives and motivations and the work I want to see done in the world also play a role. I often come across people who tell me the Morrigan is a goddess of XYZ. And I can see where they come up with that from certain parts of her lore that they find significant, or parts of the lore they are viewing in a modern sense from the perspective of modern values rather than ancient ones. But more than likely whatever they are saying she is a goddess of is an idea, concept, or cause that is close to their own hearts. That's their work in the world to champion for or understand better. Their personal work, not necessarily the deity's. The deity in question might not really care about that topic at all. The energy of that deity will likely help the priest regarding the things the priest cares about, but that doesn't change that the gods have their own agendas, and likely they are different than our own.

Managing the Expectations of Others

When you are facilitating an experience for others, whether that is a ritual, devotional, or event of some kind, it's important to be upfront about what will happen in those experiences. From the participants' viewpoint I've seen a couple of uncomfortable situations arise when those in recovery have to decide what to do when offered alcohol that was expected to be imbibed as part of a ritual, or any number of allergy issues not being taken into consideration. The spiritual agreements might be an issue when creating ritual work for large groups. It is always easier to take these into consideration when you are working with a small group that you know well. When you are serving a group in a public space that you don't know, these are important things to keep in mind. Being upfront beforehand about what your ritual will entail will help them make informed decisions.

You also can't guarantee an experience. If someone isn't blown away by a ritual you led or didn't feel a connection to the divine through it, that's not something you can control. You are there to hopefully facilitate an experience, but you can't force the gods to appear before someone. You are a bridge between the unseen and this world, but those who come to worship the gods still have to make the effort to cross that bridge.

Ego, Abusive Personalities & Abusive Leaders

In Paganism our priests are our leaders and teachers. It's a sad truth that not all of our leaders should be in those positions. Being a leader does mean a good amount of work, and that your focus is on others rather than yourself. But there are certain kinds of personalities that are attracted to the power aspect part of it. They want to be seen and listened to by others and order others around. Others want to be the mouthpieces for the gods. The thing is, you serve the gods, you aren't the gods themselves. Unfortunately, sometimes leading a group is more about an individual's personal ego trip. This of course, isn't always the case, but when you run across it, it becomes very apparent.

Just because someone else looks to a person as a leader, doesn't mean you have to. Not questioning leaders at times can be dangerous.

For example, several years ago my husband and the coven he was part of helped break up a sex cult masquerading as a Wiccan coven in Miami. The group he was practicing with were approached by the students of a man who claimed he was teaching them Wicca. From the questions they hesitantly asked, it was clear that this man was using their naiveté to take advantage of his female students. His version of Wicca involved all of his students having sex with him. The group imploded after being given accurate information about Pagan rituals and being offered support to help them disengage from their teacher. Local groups also warned others away from the man. This is an obvious abuse of leadership, but there are many more subtle abuses.

Abusive people are often charismatic and know how to groom their victims. In other cases, power goes to a person's head and they slowly become more abusive to others. The only advice I can give in these less obvious cases is speak up if leaders in your community do something you are uncomfortable with. If the situation can't be remedied, then vote with your feet and leave that group. All too often we put our leaders, authors, and teachers on pedestals. We give to them the admiration we should be offering to the gods. I'll be the first to tell you that anyone you put on a pedestal is going to disappoint you. Priests are only human and aren't perfect, and just because they have a deep connection to a deity you also have a connection with doesn't mean you'll like them on a personal level.

Very often I see people doubt their own connections to deity because someone they idolized has different points of view on mundane matters than they do. In other cases, I see priests who shun people in their communities for not holding the same opinions as they do. That can harm a community irrevocably. For example, I was at an event where the gathering was themed around honoring Celtic deities that particular year. One of the headliners was a Celtic Reconstructionist priest. Someone at the festival was very excited to meet this person and had been following their work online for many years. After a conversation with them they came back to the cabin we were sharing and were obviously very upset. Apparently, the headliner has told them that they didn't have a valid connection to the deity they worshiped because they were Wiccan. This person had looked up to this headliner, and as a result they were having a mini spiritual crisis. This person they admired said what they were doing wasn't real, or correct, because they weren't part of the same tradition as the headliner. So, they must be right? They knew better, didn't they? It made this person question if anything they experienced from deity was valid. As a priest you have to accept that others whom you might be called to serve by your gods don't hold the same views as you. They might not practice the same kind of tradition as you do, even if they honor the same god or gods. But you are not just in service to the people who agree with you. And deity isn't going speak exclusively to the people who only practice your particular path.

In many ways we have to stop looking at spirituality as a competition. Being a priest isn't about having the only right way to do things, or about other agreeing with you. Being in service to the community isn't about ruling over the community either; in many ways it is better to imagine it as helping others further themselves on their own paths. Something about our own paths can help others find fulfilment in their own. Tearing people down isn't the role of a priest; being a guidepost, a helpful ally to others seeking the presence of the gods, is.

Avoiding Burnout

Avoiding burnout is essential to public priesthood. Public work can be consuming. Often because there aren't enough people who are willing to lead events or rituals, or the more time-consuming aspects of community building. I remember going to a local Pagan monthly meetup where there was one guy who always came and threw out great ideas. Great ideas for me to do. A few of them I did, but eventually I asked him, "If you want to see that happen why don't you do it?" To which he replied it was too much work. The honest truth is people want to come to events and rituals, but they don't want to do the messy work. They don't want to organize it; they don't want to pick up the trash afterwards or get there early to set up. It isn't always the case; I do have a number of great people who have helped through the years with those tasks. But they are not in the vast majority. Cultivating a community can be hard work, but if you make helping out a mandatory part of the experience it will be helpful in instilling that in the group culture in the long run. If you are the only one running the show, doing all the things, then you are going to reach a crisis point eventually. It's how a lot of leaders and priests walk away from this kind of work. They get tired of being the only one doing things for others. You must make sure you have your own support system to lean on when you feel overwhelmed and tired. Burnout is a real thing, and I've seen a lot of priests walk away from their circles or events because of it. You have to be kind to yourself and make sure you have enough personal spiritual time to connect to the gods, balanced with your public work for them.

Priests aren't always Right

This is an important one. The reason a lot of abusive folks stay in positions of power in any religion in part is because others are afraid to call them out when they are wrong. It could be a bad decision in leadership, it could be their treatment of others within a group, or it could be something minor like a group not being able to question the priest's personal UPG. Priests are human just like the rest of us; they make mistakes. If you serve your gods as a priest or priestess, yes you too will make a mistake somewhere along the way. It's normal. This can also play into ego problems where leaders refuse to be told they are wrong about issues and bully others into either leaving or submitting to their points of view. A healthy approach to any group that you work with is to be open to criticism.

Service Isn't Glamorous

Above all a priest is a servant of the gods or spirits. Being a servant isn't glamorous. It means you are doing work. In a mundane sense it probably means you will be the first one to arrive and the last one to leave and vacuum the rental hall. The point is, the focus is on the gods and not you, so that means you won't always be doing the fun things. It also can mean a lot of time spent fundraising so certain event can happen and a lot of vacation time spent in service to the gods rather than taking it easy.

Keep Healthy Boundaries

Priests and leaders who become well known in a community can often receive some unwanted attention. Priests balance serving their community with their everyday life. We don't have a paid clergy so that means most of our priesthood are working full time jobs, raising kids, dealing with normal life issues, their own spiritual needs, and the needs of the community on top of that. That's a lot. But I've often found that some people view a priest's dedication to their community to mean that they are on call 24/7 to everyone's needs. A friend who owns a spiritual shop and hosts events in her community had someone just show up at her house out of the blue. Her kids were walking to the house from the bus, and he decided he was going to walk with them home and chat with them before demanding a reading. It's not like she wouldn't have wanted to help the person at an appropriate time. But this is someone she didn't know well, interacting with her kids as they got off the bus and showing up in her personal space not asking for a service, but demanding it. Real strong boundaries have to be established.

Similarly, I had someone contact me about a spiritual question through social media. I was at work and glanced at my phone and quickly read the message. I still had work to do and intended to answer when I got a moment in the evening if I could. A couple of hours later when I left work for the day, I saw I had another message. The person had seen that I had viewed the message and was upset that I did not reply back immediately, and since I didn't reply back right away I must not be a very spiritual person since I didn't make their request my priority. It never really occurred to them I might have a job or might be doing something in my life. I know many others who have similar stories. Keeping strong personal boundaries is important when you are a public priest. Be aware of who has your personal information, addresses, phone numbers, etc. With the magic of social media there are ways to add extra protective boundaries, have a separate page where people can contact you for your spiritual work. Not everyone in the community is safe or stable; use common sense and discretion.

Legal Issues to Consider

If you plan on officiating certain ceremonies, such as marriages, as a priest there are some legal issues to consider. In the state I live in one just needs to be a notary to officiate a marriage. I was already a notary because of my everyday job, so this was a bit simpler for me. In other states there will be different requirements. Taking the time to learn your state's laws and how you can legally officiate over certain ceremonies for your community is important. If you are traveling to do certain things, then again you need to be aware of what that those state's rules are.

Suggested Exercises

1. Take time to consider how best you can serve your local community. Identify the needs of the community and see if there are opportunities for you to be of service.

2. Identify the area in your skillset that can be improved upon. What kind of training, classes, certifications, etc. could benefit your ability to serve as a priest?

3. Reach out to experienced priests and find out what resources have been helpful to them being successful.

CHAPTER TWELVE

Oracular Work: Speaking for the Gods

The small clearing has a small fire pit at its center. Small stones outline the boundaries of the circle. The pine trees that tower over us have scattered a blanket of pine needles on the ground. As we walk on them the smell of pine rises like a kind of incense. On one side of the circle there is a large cauldron filled with water. The person who will be channeling the goddess we are honoring tonight is standing just beyond the cauldron. Another person stands behind her monitoring her trance and telling us when we can approach her.

This is one of my first experiences I have had with someone possessed by a god. I am not sure what to think, honestly. How will I know if it is really Brigid speaking to me? What will she say? Soon it is my turn to approach. The priestess anoints me with oil and some of the water from the cauldron. It is twilight and the light is strained, but what strikes me as I look at the priestess who I do know somewhat well is that she doesn't look

the same. Her hair is a slightly different shade, her eyes are differ-
ent as well. Perhaps the most startling is she is taller than me. I
am fairly tall, and I know my friend is shorter than me. But this
version of my friend is very tall, at least as tall as me. Later I
will look to see if she is standing on anything, but she is not. It is
very disconcerting. Is it an illusion? The aura of a goddess? I do
not know, but all the same she is an altered version of my friend.
She takes my hands and then she speaks. The words strike home,
things I know I have never told this person are spoken. I feel tears
running down my face. Then I am walking back to my place in the
circle. Offerings are made and the ritual continues and concludes,
but the words stay with me.

So far, our focus has been on learning to hear the voices of the gods, but when you become a priest you may do more than just connect with the divine. Sometimes the gods speak through you. This is referred to by several different names: oracular work, chan-neling, being a horse (the gods being the rider), aspecting, trance possession, and divine possession. Seidr could also be included in that list, but the term can refer both to the Norse trance practice as well as a kind of magical practice. Personally, I think possession would be the most accurate of those terms, but they all describe the same kind of work. When done correctly it can be a profoundly moving experience.

If one has an aptitude for trance work, one might even be involved in these practices before taking on the role of a priest. It's certainly possible, but more often than not one takes on this work to give the god or gods they serve a voice and to allow others to speak directly to their gods. This practice is safer when you are very well tuned to the deity you will be channeling. You should be familiar with them, have long-standing agreements, be aware of what their personalities and energies feel like before even considering letting that deity borrow your body. Because that really is what's happening. You are letting something else use your body, to speak, to touch, to feel, to act in the world. Sometimes you might have some control over your body when this is happening; other times you might be tossed in the trunk so to speak and not be aware of anything until the experience is over with. That requires trust in my opinion, and knowledge of who you are giving the keys to. You wouldn't lend your car to someone you didn't know, right? Then why would you hand the keys to your body over to a god you didn't know? Besides, gods you are not familiar with could overstep boundaries you wouldn't want to cross. If you aren't very familiar with a deity, it is also possible to let another spirit in that isn't the being you were trying to channel in the first place. Or let your higher self speak instead of deity. Simply put, a lot can go wrong.

For our purposes here we will talk about some of the things a priest must navigate when doing this work successfully. This chapter isn't going to teach you how to do trance possession. That could easily be the topic of an entire book or series of books. This is geared towards someone who already does this work and wants to improve their practices around it. Although it would be a good primer on things to avoid for someone just starting down this path as well. For more information about divine possession, I suggest reading Diana Paxson's *The Way of the Oracle* and *The Essential Guide to Possession, Depossession and Divine Relationships,* as well as my own book *Priestess of the Morrigan*. In one of the groups I work with anyone who wishes to take up practice has to go through a yearlong study course before taking this on with the group. My best advice is to be patient. It could take a year or many years of studying this practice before you feel comfortable doing it or are proficient. Much of the devotional work we have explored in the first two sections of this book would also be good groundwork building the relationship with the divine that is necessary for possession work. Some priests may never feel comfortable enough giving over control of their bodies in this way, and that is perfectly ok too.

When It Works

When divine possession works it can be a powerfully moving experience for all involved. Acting as a vessel for the gods takes its toll. It's not easy work, but it is vastly rewarding. It requires dedication and study to be able to do this practice safely. There are a lot of considerations to take when introducing this practice into a group. I really don't recommend doing this at a public event. You need to be able to ensure the person being possessed is safe. That they have at least one person with them at all times that can bring them out of trance if needed, protect their physical body, direct people as they come to speak with them, and at times tell people what is and isn't acceptable while they speak with the person channeling. You also want to make sure no outside forces try to come through or interfere with the person being possessed. For this you need time and space. The group I work with used to have a person channel during ritual in a sealed and blessed space. This is doable in a small group. But very often it could become too time consuming if we had a lot of people attend and everyone was going to the person channeling to receive a message. The ritual can easily loose its energy and flow. At bigger events we have a space set aside as a temple that is warded for the purposes of doing trance possession work. This way those who wish to ask the gods a question or seek advice can wait outside. They can be properly prepared for the process, and those who are guarding the temple can make sure no issues arise before they go into the actual temple space. However, if you wish to go about the process make sure you consider all the logistics around it. What will the space look like? How will people go in and out or speak to the possessed priest/ess? Is there anyone there to do spiritual triage if someone comes out of the experience that needs emotional support? Are you warding the space, and if so, how? There really are a whole lot of logistical things to consider, and that is very much part of what a priest does too.

Entering Trance

This is a topic that can fill an entire book, and indeed several books have been written about it. To be able to channel deity you need to be really dedicated to working on meditation practices. You need to be able to go into a deep meditative state and maintain it for a prolonged period of time, most likely while moving or standing. Practicing moving meditations would be a good starting point. Creating trance triggers, words, music, or a pattern you draw on your hand, or even putting on special makeup that signals your mind to enter a meditative or trance state will be helpful as well. Whatever your process is, you need to know it backward and forward and be able to do it successfully. This takes practice and time spent on refining these skills daily. In addition to that you must spend time connecting to the deity you will channel, know their energy, and be able to identify them.

Some people prefer to visualize themselves stepping into the energy or shape of a god. Like they are stepping into their form and merging with them, others may see deity filling and possessing them differently. Energetically when this happens the person's aura may appear larger, physical appearances may look different or hard to focus on. If you can imagine the energetic fields of an aura as a layer cake, it would look something like every other layer is either the god's energy or the person channeling. Something to consider about channeling or possession work is that by sharing your body and energy with deity, you start to become more like them energetically. It's kind of like an imprint on your energetic fields. This isn't necessarily a bad thing but can have unforeseen consequences. In part this is why I only channel, in the sense of full-on possession, deities that I have a strong devotional relationship with. They already are an integral part of my life and I want them there. Because even when deity leaves, some part of that divine pattern still stays imprinted for a while. If you want that, then there isn't a problem. But if you don't, or you only want to channel X deity on Beltane because you think it works well for the ritual, well maybe think about how closely you want your energies entwined with that deity.

When It Goes Wrong

When it goes wrong it can go epically wrong. Having a tight-knit group that knows how and when to step in is always helpful. But making mistakes is also how we learn. You are going to make mistakes. Make peace with that; it's just how life works. Having a plan regarding who will step in when something is going sideways will be immensely helpful. There are several things that can go wrong. The gods might not want to speak. When that happens don't force it; change the ritual or postpone and try at another time or day. If the gods don't want to speak, then you can't do anything about it. The person channeling might have just had something traumatic or upsetting going on in their personal life. If they aren't in the right headspace, then they need to sit out and have someone else take their place. We all have bad days; don't be afraid to admit it. Another scenario is something else comes through that isn't the deity you intended. I've only had this happen once and it's not pretty. When this happened, I invited a person who I knew did channeling work to be part of a ritual. They didn't really do their research on the aspect of the deity we were going to call upon for the ritual. They came to me asking a few quick questions about the deity right before the ritual was going to start. Red flag, but I thought, well they know what they are doing, they have done this kind of work before. They know what they are doing. Sure, they had done this work before, but they didn't prepare, and I should have shut it down right then and there. During the ritual they were channeling something, but not the aspect they thought they were. As far as most of us could tell since that deity was connected to the Faery Folk, we were fairly sure the person accidently let in a faery being. The energy was all wrong; the person wasn't in control and eventually I had to shut the ritual down. People weren't happy about it, but it was the safer things to do. The next day we all spent time making offerings and appeasing the gods and doing some spiritual triage work to make sure it didn't happen again. Go with your guts; if something is wrong you need to make sure everyone is safe, both those present and those channeling. If you need to stop then you stop. Talk with the other priests in your group, have a game plan about how to handle situations that go sideways. Having everyone on board with how to handle a bad situation will go a long way to being able to handle issues when they arise.

Support Crew

In my own work we call the support crew of priests who help facilitate possession work "guardians." Whatever you wish to call these folks, they are essential to your success. There should be at least one priest who is the guardian for the priest who is channeling. They are the one who attends to the priest's physical needs while they aren't in control of their bodies. That might be making sure they drink water when needed or making sure they eat something and help them ground after they are done channeling. In other cases, it might be to help them come out of trance, as well as ward the space from disruptive energies. Disruptive energies can be anything from outside spirits or the energies of the people coming to speak with the person channeling. They will also be the ones to make sure everyone entering the space knows how to act and what to do during the experience. They are also your first line of defense in making sure someone who isn't in the right headspace or is inebriated doesn't get into the temple space.

Handling Ego Trips

Part of why it is important to not rush into this kind of work is because it is really easy for your ego to become a problem. You really have to know yourself. The good, the bad, and the ugly and be at peace with who you are. If you are going through some difficult personal stuff or your life is a hot mess, then channeling isn't something you should be doing until the rest of your life is in order. That goes for folks who have been doing this for a long time too. First off, it is very hard to come back to yourself and be fully possessed of yourself after possession work if you don't know who the heck you are or if your emotions are all over the place. It will also be pretty hard to let the divine within yourself because of those reasons. In the worse scenarios someone in this state probably won't be channeling the divine at all and will be letting their own personal biases come through instead of the gods. They may be doing this without even realizing it too.

The other side of this is someone who is attracted to this kind of work because they want to be special. They want people fawning over them and thanking them for passing on the messages of the gods or asking them for personal readings. This is also a sign of an ego out of check. I've seen a lot of these. These are the folks who channel big ominous messages and relay them very publicly, reminding everyone that they have the direct hotline to the gods, and they have been told to tell community to do XYZ, and no one is allowed to question them. They might also have a message that fits exactly with their own personal agendas or ideologies. This can be dangerous. Once they have a group of people believing they have the gods on speed dial then nothing they say or do can be questioned, especially when they bully others or indulge in abusive behavior. The problem is if people call them on their bad behavior then they feel that the inspiring messages they received from that person must be false too. Unfortunately, most people would rather overlook a leader's bad behavior than call them on doing something inappropriate. The thing is a channel is just a vessel, they could tell you accurate information, because it isn't them tell you the information anyway it's the god speaking through them, and still be a horrible person. Why would the gods use a bad person as their vessel? Well, in my experience the gods want to speak to us, and sometimes we aren't very good at listening. I think they will take any opportunity offered to them to speak, if they want to do so, regardless of whether the person is acting as the vessel. Sometimes you get to drive around in a Lamborghini and sometimes you got to settle for the beater Honda. And the honest truth is sometimes good people do bad things. They go on ego trips, they don't know how to handle being in leadership roles, they let being praised go to their heads, or they feel they can use them as their own personal platforms. But what this kind of behavior does is inexcusable. It can lead to others being disillusioned and questions their faith and connection to the gods, and it's a betrayal of trust. The job of a priest is to nip this kind of behavior in the bud. Trust what others tell you if bad behavior is being reported. Usually it will become clear fairly quickly if someone is interested in this work for the wrong reasons or can't control their ego well enough to be a good fit for this work.

The Message Addict

Whether you are doing this in a small personal group or doing it in a larger community, it is a good idea to have more than one person acting as the oracle. If you only have one person who does this work a lot of times the community starts seeing them as a hotline to the gods. They forget that the person who is relaying these very personal messages from the gods isn't the gods themselves. They are only the vessel, and most of the time they probably don't even remember the conversation that happened when the god was running the show. For myself what I remember feels like a dream. I know I saw people and they spoke to me and I spoke to them, but other than the vaguest of feelings I don't know what I said. Usually what I pick up the most on is, how the deity I was holding space for within myself felt when they talked to them. My awareness is really all consumed with keeping the phone line open and keeping my body upright while deity does their thing if I'm aware of anything at all. That being said, if someone only experiences one person doing this work, they start to elevate them in their minds. This is the special person who speaks to the gods for me, who knows all the answers. Sometimes people can get very demanding asking for that person to channel for them on demand. Or they might forget to do their own practices and see this person as their only avenue of communication to the divine, when if they listened hard enough, they could probably get their own answers from the gods. In Seidr the person in trance has a veil over their heads, which in many cases means you might not know who the vessel of the gods is. Similarly, I use a long scarf that covers most of my face. Sensory deprivation can be helpful in inducing trance, and personally it has become a kind of trigger to get myself into that headspace. The additional benefit is that the person I am speaking to in trance doesn't see much of my face, and depending on the circumstance may not even know who I am. That in addition to having several people who rotate doing this practice can help alleviate unhealthy hero worship. Also, channeling can take a toll on the physical body if done for too long. Think about how long you expect the person channeling to stay in trance if doing this in a ritual setting. If you are doing it in a more controlled setting, such as a temple or room set aside solely for this work, consider having a few people rotate through this role so you do not wear anyone out.

Setting the Stage

When offering this kind of work to the community it's important to set up expectations for those who will ask questions or interact with the person who is possessed. African Traditional Religions and the Heathen Seidr are some of the few that still practice this regularly, which means that most Pagans haven't been around someone who is possessed. This means there is a big learning curve. Most folks won't know how they are expected to act or what is or isn't appropriate unless you relay that info to them. I have had folk who once in front of the channel ask for healing or soul retrieval when they were only supposed to ask a question of the channel. Healing and soul retrieval, besides being something that would not take a few minutes, was also not something we had set the space up for. Others have taken it as their own private session where they want to ask the oracle fifty questions when there are others waiting for their few minutes in the presence of the gods. At some semiprivate gatherings I've had people show up drunk wishing to speak to the oracle that had to be turned away. Others treat it as a parlor trick and are upset if the gods didn't tell them what they wanted to hear or perhaps didn't have a message for them. The gods don't work on demand; sometimes they don't have anything to say to someone and that has to be respected. You can't force a god to offer profound wisdom to someone on demand.

The best way to combat issues such as these is to make it very clear that those coming to speak with the person channeling are only there to ask a question. Have them spend some time as they are waiting to think of the question they want to ask, to refine it and clarify it in their heads. If you have a temple space set up where people go in to see the person channeling one at a time, have them sit and meditate on their question, and help them walk through some grounding and centering exercises. Also tell them what to expect when they are in front of the person channeling. Can they touch them? Should they wait for the channel to take their hand? Will there be someone there to lead them to the person channeling? Will they be able to make an offering before or after they ask their question in the temple space? Is there anything they shouldn't do? All of this is important information you should be conveying to folks before they are around someone who isn't in control of their body. It also means you need a really good support staff. For this kind of work to go well you don't just need someone who is proficient in trance possession, but also a dedicated team to help protect that person, and make the process move smoothly with those seeking the experience.

Finding Your Way Back

Trance isn't something that can be turned on and off at the flip of a switch. Using triggers to help you go into trance can speed up the process, but just as it takes a concentrated effort to enter trance, so too does it take an effort to come back to your body.

Having a good support staff will aid in this process. If everything is running smoothly the guardian should be the one keeping an eye on the time and the condition of the priest channeling. Are they swaying on their feet? Do you sense something is wrong energetically? The majority of the time when I am in trance time is somewhat meaningless. An hour can feel like five minutes to me.

My body on the other hand will disagree with me once I'm fully aware of it again because it has been standing for an hour while I wasn't quite there. Again, this means to successfully do this kind of work you need help, ideally someone you work well with magically and trust to watch out for your needs. Having a signal indicating that you need to stop is also a good idea. It can be something simple, a gesture or word, that only your guardian knows.

In general when I end trance it is very much like beginning it, just in reverse. There is a mental communication between deity and myself that it is now time to end the work we are doing. I see deity leaving my body. Some people like to visualize this as the deity stepping in or out of their physical body or seeing their energy moving away from you. Next, I reaffirm the boundaries of my own being. This is something that will be different for everyone. You need to be intimately aware of what your energy feels like. What are the boundaries and geography of your spirit? Where do your energies begin and end? Again, that is something that takes practice, both to close those spiritual borders down, and to open them in the first place to let deity in. After I have established all the remaining energy is my own, and I have pushed out anything that is not, I begin to ground myself. Grounding for myself begins with saying my names, all of them, magical and otherwise. They define who I am in this life and doing so helps me become fully grounded in my body and my own awareness. Lastly offerings are made to the deity that has been speaking through me.

If a priest has been in trance too long and their body needs the trance to end, such as when a guardian notices they are swaying or there is some other sign of trouble, this is also when a guardian should intervene. This could also be if they have lost control and can't successfully return to their body. In both these scenarios the guardian working with the priest would need to intervene. They may energetically need to push the deity out of the priest's body or speak with the god or spirit asking them to leave. In general, I find if asked directly deity will go. Gods always remember that we have limits or need to drink water or can't stand for hours on end. The guardian helping to ground the priest's energies can be helpful in coming out of trance and well as aftercare for any trance work.

Suggested Exercises

1. Spend some time journaling or meditating on what draws you to this work.

2. Create a statement of purpose for your work. This can be something that you go back to look at often and helps focus why you are taking on your oracular practice.

3. Identify other resources that will help you in this work. That can be other experienced practitioners, books, courses, or other training.

A Ritual of Priesthood

You Will Need

Vows of priesthood you have written

Anointing oil

An offering of your choice

A ritual of dedication as a priest is highly personal. There can be no cookie cutter format to it, only examples to help you create what will be right for you. Use this ritual to help you in forming your own. As with the ritual of dedication you should spend a least the week before or longer doing devotional work, connecting with deity and creating your vow as a priest. We have already discussed how important oaths and vows are, and a vow of priesthood and all it entails is especially so. Choose your words wisely and feel out what deity expects and wants regarding priesthood. If you are part of a group or tradition that will be recognizing you as clergy this will likely be a group effort, and they will be witness to your vows.

The offering you give for taking on this role should also be significant. Again, that does not mean expensive or excessive, but instead meaningful to you and appropriate for the deity.

Begin your ritual in whatever manner you chose. When you are ready hold your hands over the anointing oil you have chosen, saying:

> *May the blessings and grace of* (name of deity)
> *flow through and be with me this day*

Anoint your forehead, hands and feet with a little bit of the oil, saying:

> *May I know your wisdom* (anoint forehead)
> *May I do your work* (anoint hands)
> *May I walk with you at my side always* (anoint feet)

Spend some time inviting in the presence of deity. If there is a chant or prayer you wish to use to invite their presence for this ritual, do so. When you are ready, say:

(Name of deity), *I who am your child,*
your humble servant, call to you!
May the words I speak reach your ears
May they be accepted and made sacred in your name!

At this point say your oath. Do not rush this part; take your time, see your words reaching out through the worlds to deity. When you are ready make your offering.

With this offering I seal my vow,
(Name of deity), *may it be worthy of you and accepted!*

At this point you may wish to do some divination or have another person present confirm your vow and offering has been accepted. Also, this is a good time to do divination or let yourself be open to any messages deity may wish to relay to you.

Close the ritual in whatever manner you chose.

Conclusion

Everyone's journey with the gods is different. For some being devoted to a deity will define their path, others might feel the gods calling them to priesthood, and yet others might find they are dedicants, serving the gods in their own way. There are many paths and many branches to divine connection. We may fill several roles throughout our journeys, yet at the core we are all doing the same thing, reaching out to the divine, seeking to make the presence and voices of the gods a part of our lives. The gods are waiting for us to learn how to hear their voices. However you see or serve them our relationships with the unseen can change the course of our lives. Connecting with the divine, in all its varied forms and guises, is at the heart of any spiritual practice. It is what helps us get through dark times in our lives, helps us face challenges, and helps us find meaning and direction in life.

So much about connecting to the divine is about your personal journey. No two people approach a devotional relationship exactly the same way. It is something that can take a lifetime for us to explore. What is important, no matter where you find yourself at the end of the journey, is that you sought out that divine connection in the first place.

Devotion was something that I stumbled through for a long time. I knew that the gods were there, but learning to speak their language, to know how to approach them was something I had to feel out on my own. I didn't have a road map. I hope this book has been that road map for you that will help you on your own journey. May the gods speak to you with clarity, and may their wisdom guide you in all that you do.

Bibliography

Apollonios Rhodios. Green, Peter, trans. *Argonautica*. Berkeley, CA: University of California Press, 2008.

Bellows, Henry Adams. *The Poetic Edda*. Princeton: Princeton University Press, 1936.

Benediktsson, Jakob, trans. *Íslendingabók, Landnámabók*. Hið Íslenzka Fornritafélag, 1968.

Brown, Nimue. *When A Pagan Prays: Exploring Prayer in Druidry and Beyond*. Winchester: Moon Books, 2014.

Daimler, Morgan. "Priesthood in Service to the Other—Part 1: The Wide View." Living Liminally (blog), May 10, 2019 https://lairbhan.blogspot.com/2019/05/priesthood-in-service-to-other.html.

———. *Where the Hawthorn Grows*. Winchester: Moon Books, 2013.

Faraday, L. W. *The Cattle Raid of Cualnge*. London: David Nutt, 1904.

Gerrard, Katie. *Seidr: The Gate is Open*. London: BM Avalonia, 2011.

Homer. Calverley, Charles Stuart, trans. *Homer's Iliad: The Iliad of Homer Volume 1*. University of Virginia: G. Bell, 1909.

Krasskova, Galina. *Devotional Polytheism: An Introduction*. CreateSpace Independent Publishing Platform, 2014.

———. *A Modern Guide to Heathenry: Lore, Celebrations, and Mysteries of the Northern Traditions*. Newburyport: Weiser Books, 2019.

MacAlister, R.A.S, trans. *Lebor Gabala Erenn: The Book of the Taking of Ireland*. Dublin: Irish Text Society, 1956.

Matthews, John. *Taliesin: The Last Celtic Shaman*. Rochester: Inner Traditions, 1991.

Ovid, and Charles Martin, trans. *Metamorphoses: A New Translation*. New York: W. W. Norton & Company, 2005.

Thomas, Kirk. *Sacred Gifts: Reciprocity and the Gods*. Tucson: ADF Publishing, 2015.

Valunos, Lucy. *One Heat, Many Gods: The Absolute Beginner's Guide to Devotional Polytheism*. Amazon.com Services LLC, 2016.